$\mathcal{I}$SAIAH

Trusting God
in Troubled Times

22 studies
for individuals or groups

Howard Peskett

With Notes for Leaders

ivp

InterVarsity Press
Downers Grove, Illinois

InterVarsity Press
P.O. Box 1400, Downers Grove, IL 60515-1426
World Wide Web: www.ivpress.com
E-mail: mail@ivpress.com

InterVarsity Press® *is the book-publishing division of InterVarsity Christian Fellowship/USA*®*, a student movement active on campus at hundreds of universities, colleges and schools of nursing in the United States of America, and a member movement of the International Fellowship of Evangelical Students. For information about local and regional activities, write Public Relations Dept., InterVarsity Christian Fellowship/USA, 6400 Schroeder Rd., P.O. Box 7895, Madison, WI 53707-7895.*

Cover photograph: Dennis Flaherty

ISBN 0-8308-3029-4

Printed in the United States of America

19   18   17   16   15   14   13   12   11   10   9   8   7   6   5   4

Contents

Getting the Most Out of *Isaiah*

Tragedies rarely come with rehearsal time. When the earthquake strikes, the quality of the buildings is revealed. A lot of life is humdrum and routine. Lifelong habits are hard to change. Two verses have struck me with great force as I have revised these Bible studies. *I will trust and not flap.* This is my personalized version of the last phrase of Isaiah 28:16. A student at the college where I preached on this text quoted it back at me some months later when I was showing signs of stress! Memorizing this verse, talking about it and even preaching on it are one thing. Having this text embedded in my deepest consciousness so that my life incarnates the peacefulness it describes is something else. How then does transformation occur? Here is where the second verse comes in.

In returning and rest you will be saved; in quietness and trust will be your strength. It is possible for us to interpret these words from Isaiah 30:15 in a way that is too cozy and comfortable—a few night lights, some sweet, sentimental songs, a bit of psychological massage and ego affirmation, and all will be well. But Isaiah is calling for something more radical—a change of mind and heart, repentance, *metanoia*. The word *returning* is commonly used for repentance in the Old Testament. It means to turn around, to turn back, to about turn. If you have taken a wrong turn, the best way forward, the most progressive decision you can make, may be to turn back.

Both of these texts come from a time of major international crisis for the small kingdom of Judah, tottering on the edge of the Western Asian world in the eighth century before Christ and on the brink of being invaded by the world superpower of the day, Assyria. Judah's leaders were doubtful that "trusting in God," as Isaiah counseled, was very practical in the circumstances. An alliance with Egypt, with their great new military breakthrough (cavalry!) seemed much more promising. Isaiah's quiet faith did not mean he minced his words! He called this policy a ramshackle refuge of lies and death that would be swept away by a flood (28:15, 17-19). He called it a bed that was too short and a duvet that was too narrow—a recipe for a long night of frustration and sleeplessness (28:20).

He called the wheelers and dealers at Judah's helm a bulging wall about to collapse (30:13), a piece of pottery about to be smashed so thoroughly that there would not even be a teaspoon-sized fragment left (30:14). They think that Egyptian cavalry is the answer, do they? Alright, ride they will—but in pell-mell flight, a thousand before one! Far from being the secret of victory, Judah will be left like a mobile phone mast, alone in a deserted landscape.

God has one foundation for peace of mind and heart, and we have another. The people said "No" to Isaiah's message, and so their hopes were deferred—toward a king who would reign in righteousness (32:1) and toward the pouring out of the Holy Spirit from on high (32:15). God's foundation rock is (according to Isaiah) tested, precious and sure. Later this Rock is revealed to be a Person, whose faithfulness stretches right down the line to laying down his life for us. Every word of God proves true and he will do all that he has promised.

It is sobering to reflect that centuries and a much fuller revelation later, we still have a hard time living lives of radical personal trust. There is a lot wrong about our society as well—things which will not be put right by parties of the right *or* the left. What is needed is parties of the Underground! People who will pay attention to the foundations of society and on what our most cherished values rest. Polls show that millions of people believe in some sort of god, gods or God. But it doesn't make any difference to their lives. Here is the difference between "believing that . . ." and decisive, life-changing trustfulness which is able to keep us going through all the changes and chances of life, against all the "slings and arrows of outrageous fortune."

These studies are written as fertilizer for that sort of trustfulness. May it sprout and grow far and wide. May our lives be wonderfully enriched and deepened as we discover more and more how utterly trustable our God is. I still remember Eugene Kwa and the first time I developed these studies for his church members after his death from cancer in 1983 at a very early age. This is why I have dedicated these studies to his wife, Ann Nai, and the members of the church which he pastored.

Why Isaiah?
Why should we study Isaiah? We should study Isaiah both because it is part of Holy Scripture and because it is great literature. We should study Isaiah because it is very frequently quoted or alluded to in the

New Testament. We should study these selected passages because trusting God is still essential and troubled times are our lot too.

These studies contain some fascinating passages, including
☐ hard-hitting criticisms of empty religion
☐ panoramic and extraordinarily impressive views of God's coming day of judgment and the everlasting joys that follow it
☐ some of the most famous Messianic prophecies
☐ dramatic narratives of times of national crisis
☐ honest exposures of a rotten society and a heartfelt cry for revival
☐ the famous story of Isaiah's call and mysterious commission and meditations on what it means for us to be trustful, faithful servants of God
☐ robust assertions that God is the world's only Savior with worldwide purposes that we are to fulfill
☐ many passages full of pastoral comfort and memorable verses for our "spiritual armory"

Trusting God in Troubled Times
Isaiah lived through turbulent times. He was called to his work at a time when a famous Assyrian king was building his empire into the largest and cruelest that western Asia had ever seen. He saw the neighboring kingdom of Israel crack, collapse and vanish in a maelstrom of intrigue, assassination, siege, deportation and imprisonment. It is in this same region that we have recently seen a very fierce war involving Iraq, Israel and many other countries around the world.

For forty years Isaiah was a king's advisor, walking quietly in the corridors of power and challenging a knock-kneed king to trust God. He encouraged this tearful king to trust God when he himself could see the campfires of the apparently invincible Assyrian army right outside his own city's locked gates and hear the crude and roaring threats of the Assyrian general coming over the walls.

We know nothing of Isaiah's wife, but he had two sons with names that were signposts to coming events. Isaiah was a social critic, remorselessly applying the yardstick of God's law to what he saw. He was a prophet—not an astrologer with cunningly ambiguous forecasts, but a man who saw both the present and the future in an eternal light. He was a pastor, or a shepherd, looking with compassion on his fellow citizens and feeding them by teaching them. He was a poet, seeing the same things and events as others, but seeing them more fully, more deeply, more sharply.

It is our privilege to read his words, to be still, to observe, to receive, to meditate on what he said, and then to join in life-building, invigorating discussion in order that we too might trust God more, and thus with joy draw water from the wells of salvation.

Isaiah's hundred pages represent forty years of ministry. What then is his unusual impact? Most of the time *he lived what he talked.* And this too must be our aim. As we study together, we want our lives to find a still center and quiet eloquence in the strength of Isaiah's words.

"This is what the Sovereign LORD, the Holy One of Israel, says: 'In repentance and rest is your salvation, in quietness and trust is your strength'" (Isaiah 30:15).

Suggestions for Individual Study

1. As you begin each study, pray that God will speak to you through his Word.

2. Read the introduction to the study and respond to the personal reflection question or exercise. This is designed to help you focus on God and on the theme of the study.

3. Each study deals with a particular passage—so that you can delve into the author's meaning in that context. Read and reread the passage to be studied. If you are studying a book, it will be helpful to read through the entire book prior to the first study. The questions are written using the language of the New International Version, so you may wish to use that version of the Bible. The New Revised Standard Version is also recommended.

4. This is an inductive Bible study, designed to help you discover for yourself what Scripture is saying. The study includes three types of questions. *Observation* questions ask about the basic facts: who, what, when, where and how. *Interpretation* questions delve into the meaning of the passage. *Application* questions help you discover the implications of the text for growing in Christ. These three keys unlock the treasures of Scripture.

Write your answers to the questions in the spaces provided or in a personal journal. Writing can bring clarity and deeper understanding of yourself and of God's Word.

5. It might be good to have a Bible dictionary handy. Use it to look up any unfamiliar words, names or places.

6. Use the prayer suggestion to guide you in thanking God for what you have learned and to pray about the applications that have come to mind.

7. You may want to go on to the suggestion under "Now or Later," or you may want to use that idea for your next study.

Suggestions for Members of a Group Study

1. Come to the study prepared. Follow the suggestions for individual study mentioned above. You will find that careful preparation will greatly enrich your time spent in group discussion.

2. Be willing to participate in the discussion. The leader of your group will not be lecturing. Instead, he or she will be encouraging the members of the group to discuss what they have learned. The leader will be asking the questions that are found in this guide.

3. Stick to the topic being discussed. Your answers should be based on the verses which are the focus of the discussion and not on outside authorities such as commentaries or speakers. These studies focus on a particular passage of Scripture. Only rarely should you refer to other portions of the Bible. This allows for everyone to participate in in-depth study on equal ground.

4. Be sensitive to the other members of the group. Listen attentively when they describe what they have learned. You may be surprised by their insights! Each question assumes a variety of answers. Many questions do not have "right" answers, particularly questions that aim at meaning or application. Instead the questions push us to explore the passage more thoroughly.

When possible, link what you say to the comments of others. Also, be affirming whenever you can. This will encourage some of the more hesitant members of the group to participate.

5. Be careful not to dominate the discussion. We are sometimes so eager to express our thoughts that we leave too little opportunity for others to respond. By all means participate! But allow others to also.

6. Expect God to teach you through the passage being discussed and through the other members of the group. Pray that you will have an enjoyable and profitable time together, but also that as a result of the study you will find ways that you can take action individually and/or as a group.

7. Remember that anything said in the group is considered confidential and should not be discussed outside the group unless specific permission is given to do so.

8. If you are the group leader, you will find additional suggestions at the back of the guide.

1

No More
Rotten Religion!

Isaiah 1

Squeeze out the Power of God.
Soul becomes empty
Church becomes dead.

Someone once said, "The history of religious movements is: Man—Movement—Monument." Why do you think that there is a tendency for religious movements to become formal, empty, ritualized and, finally, fossilized?

GROUP DISCUSSION. What signs do you see in your society of both plentiful religiosity and moral evils among the same people? How is it that these things can coexist?

PERSONAL REFLECTION. Now do you detect phony religiosity in yourself and in others?

If you were writing your biography, how would you begin? Birth? We might expect the book of Isaiah to begin with the prophet's call, but this doesn't come until chapter 6. Why not? The most probable answer is that before we can understand Isaiah's confession and the Lord's strange commission in chapter 6, we must understand something of the society in which Isaiah lived and to which he was called to preach. *Read Isaiah 1.*

---

1. In verses 2-3 the Lord summons heaven and earth to be witnesses of his accusations against his people. What is the impact of the two

Symbol-comparison

metaphors the Lord uses to describe his people's unreasonable and rebellious conduct?

---

2. Both the nation (v. 4) and the country (v. 7) are in a shocking condition. What vivid pictures of sinfulness do verses 4-9 provide?

Iniquity, offspring of evildoers, corrupted sons, forsaken the Lord, spiritually enemies taken over theirdand, physically dead, dead!

3. Notice how many times is rebellion mentioned in this chapter. Why do people turn their backs on One who loves them?

! Ccause they think they no more

4. These people who verses 2-9 speak of were religious! How does God react in verses 10-15 to all of their religious commotion?

---

5. Describe the kind of life that God is asking them to lead instead (vv. 16-17).

Put away the old man + Put on the new man taking care of Bod

6. From your own experience, explain why it is much harder to fulfill the moral requirements of verses 16-17 than just to go through the ritual activities mentioned in verses 10-15. *James 4:7*

---

7. Pass over verses 18-20 for the moment and look at verses 21-26. You will notice that these verses are framed by reference to "the faithful city" (Jerusalem or Zion). Life in the capital reflects life in the nation. What picture do these verses give of life in Jerusalem?

8. God's judgment is compared in verses 25-31 to a refining (v. 25) and destroying (v. 31) fire. How does the phrase "redeemed with justice" (v. 27) highlight the connection of salvation to a changed life?

9. Now return to verses 18-20. Some scholars think verse 18 is a cynical question, but traditionally it has been understood as a gracious invitation by humanity's Accuser and Judge. What does this invitation offer?

What does it threaten?

10. What reorientation does your life require if your religion is not to be just a burden—to you and to God?

Give thanks to our wonderful Lord, who can wash out fast colors and delete the indelible.

Now or Later

Before you read this chapter, how would you have defined a "scarlet sin"?

From this chapter, what sins would you say God views as scarlet?

2

Longing & Living for *That Day*

Isaiah 2

Standing outside the Old City of Jerusalem (in what used to be no-man's land) is one of the most poignant memorials in Israel to the Six Day War in 1967. It is a futuristic sculpture made of wrecked military equipment with words from Isaiah chapter 2 on it: "They will beat their swords into plowshares and their spears into pruning hooks. Nation will not take up sword against nation, nor will they train for war any more" (v. 4).

GROUP DISCUSSION. When you read the quote above and think of the current state of affairs in our world, how do you respond?

PERSONAL REFLECTION. Ponder a time when you have been most conscious of "the splendor of God's majesty." What sort of feelings did that involve? ⌐

Actors rehearse for their performances. Skydivers watch the weather. Pianists practice for their concerts. Athletes train for the Olympics. For what "day" do believers long, prepare, live? And how do they prepare? *Read Isaiah 2.*

---

1. To what period or periods do the words *day* and *days* refer (vv. 2, 11-12, 17, 20)?

2. What distinguishes the mountain of the Lord (v. 2) at Jerusalem is certainly not its altitude. It is lower than Hebron and much lower than Hermon. What then is its qualification to be the "chief" that makes other higher mountains look on enviously?

3. The nations stream toward Jerusalem to learn the Lord's ways and paths. How do you maintain this essential balance of learning and doing in your life?

4. What would you do if you knew the world would end next week?

5. Verse 3 pictures people streaming in and God's word spreading out. How do you share in getting God's message out?

6. Verses 6-9 provide a rather sad contrast to the vision of verses 2-4. What is the land full of according to these verses?

7. Verses 10-21 mention a number of great things, some natural, some human and some manufactured, which will be brought low in the day when the splendor of God's majesty is revealed. What things are specifically mentioned?

8. What hints do verses 9 and 22 give regarding God's purposes in this day of reversals?

---

9. How would your life change if you were to be more continually conscious of the Lord and the "splendor of his majesty"?

---

10. What incentives and encouragements do chapters 1 and 2 of Isaiah give you to trust God in troubled times?

Pray the first three petitions of the Lord's prayer and then stop and reflect what is involved in the words "on earth as it is in heaven."

Now or Later

---

11. *Read Isaiah 3—4*, which forms a bridge to our next study. Jerusalem and Judah have been "defying the Lord's glorious presence" (3:8). What will happen to the structure of their society when the Lord arises to judge the people?

---

12. In 3:16—4:1 a fashion parade (twenty-one items of female finery are mentioned) comes to a tragic end. What modern obsessions hinder us from attending to the splendor of the Lord's majesty?

---

13. Beyond the coming judgment there is a bright prospect: new growth, holiness, cleansing, light, glory. How have you found the protection of the Lord's presence (4:6) refreshing in your own experience?

3

A Song
of Injustice

Isaiah 5

Many modern songs are about real or perceived injustices. Why are these protests often cast in the form of songs?

GROUP DISCUSSION. "Be sure your sins will find you out." This may seem like a quaint saying, but what examples can you give of how you've seen it to be true?

PERSONAL REFLECTION. Recall a song (sacred or secular) which has deeply moved you. Why and in what direction?

The setting of this chapter of Isaiah was probably during the grape harvest, a famous time for conversation and conviviality. Isaiah uses a short parable to rouse his friends' consciences, and then with mounting vehemence he attacks certain sins directly. *Read Isaiah 5.*

---

1. Choosing carefully the occasion and form (a love song), Isaiah introduces the subject of a dear friend's vineyard. Describe the care that was lavished on the vineyard and the owner's dismay when the final product was only evil-smelling, bitter, wild grapes.

2. Verses 3 and 5, both beginning with the word *now*, invite the listeners' verdict on the vineyard. What is the owner's decision about what to do with the vineyard (vv. 5-6)?

---

3. Dropping the disguise of the parable, Isaiah rams home the lesson to his people directly in verse 7. Contrast what God looked for among his people with what he found.

---

4. Have you ever been in a situation in which you needed to confront a friend with inconsistencies in his or her lifestyle? What happened?

---

5. Give examples of ways in which God has lavished his care on you or on your society, only to be rewarded by a bitter harvest.

---

6. Verses 8-23 fall into six sections introduced by the word *woe*. What are the sins described in each of these sections?

---

7. What do these woes reveal about the society at this time?

How do you find your own society mirrored in these verses?

8. What is the real objection to the conduct revealed in these verses? (See especially vv. 12 and 24.)

9. What punishment does the Lord announce in verses 9-10, 13-17 and 24-25?

10. The nation from afar, which God summons with a whistle in verse 26, is the world superpower of those days—Assyria. What impression do you gain of their army in verses 26-30?

11. If you are not rich and influential you may be able to dissociate yourself from the sins described here. But what ways do we have of ignoring God's works (v. 12) and acting as if things are never going to change, least of all by divine intervention (v. 19)?

Pray for one sweet fruit to grow in the vineyard of your life, which God has tended so lovingly.

Now or Later
Write a short poem on the state of your society. You might like to use the form of a haiku—three unrhymed lines of five, seven and five syllables.

4

Responding to God's Call

Isaiah 6

Holiness is a controversial quality. A few saints get to have icon status in the community at large, but many are ignored or derided; some are persecuted and martyred.

GROUP DISCUSSION. What reverberations does the word *holy* set off in your mind? What appeal does it have, and what demands does it make?

PERSONAL REFLECTION. We commonly think that only pastors and missionaries need a "call" from God. What is the difference between a vocation and a career?

In this chapter Isaiah comes before the presence of God. He is so overcome by the experience that he cries out, "Woe to me!" God is gracious to Isaiah, however, and gives him a special mission. Through this famous story we will learn something about God's call to us also. *Read Isaiah 6.*

1. Uzziah's long and prosperous reign came to an end under a cloud (see 2 Chronicles 26:16-21). What do you think was Isaiah's purpose in verse 1 in describing God as occupying the throne?

2. Describe as vividly as possible what Isaiah saw (vv. 2-4).

3. What is the significance of the seraphs' song (v. 3) in the context of the state of Isaiah's society and his own call?

What resulted from their song (v. 4)?

4. Annie Dillard said that we should put on a crash helmet and seat belts when we go to worship God. Have you ever been really shaken up by a sense of God's presence and holiness? What happened?

5. What is the significance of Isaiah's cry in verse 5, especially his reference to his own and his people's lips?

6. What wonderful answer did Isaiah get to his cry of pain (vv. 6-7)?

7. Smell the burning flesh of verse 7. What might it mean for you to belong to the FBL (the Fellowship of Burnt Lips)?

8. Note God's request and Isaiah's response in verse 8. How do you think Isaiah felt at this point?

9. In verses 8-10, Isaiah receives his call. If we follow the punctuation in the New International Version very carefully, it appears that verse 9 is what Isaiah is to tell the people, and verse 10 is God's summary of what will happen. Describe what Isaiah's ministry will be like.

---

10. Isaiah persevered in his prophetic work for decades. What will help you to persevere in your witness despite opposition and apathy?

---

11. Isaiah's surprisingly cool response to this commission is to inquire how long he should continue (v. 11). What is God's answer to this question (vv. 11-13)?

---

12. Responding to God's call in a stirring moment can be a powerful and energizing memory. How does hope continually rekindle that response and keep it fresh?

Pray for a fresh vision of God's holiness and forgiveness to kindle your steady obedience to his call.

Now or Later

"Despair and presumption are two kinds of hopelessness. Of hope's fulfillment despair says, 'Never!' and presumption says, 'Already!'" (Josef Pieper, *On Hope*, trans. Mary Frances McCarthy [San Francisco: Ignatius Press, 1986], p. 47). Reflect on encouraging examples of steadfastness that you know, and ponder how you too may walk steadily along the high, hard path of hope.

5

To Us a Child
Is Born

Isaiah 8:19—9:7

Total darkness is disorientating; you lose your sense of time and space; hallucinations and even insanity may follow. Why does light affect us so deeply?

GROUP DISCUSSION. Why are astrology and other pagan spiritual practices so attractive to millions of people?

PERSONAL REFLECTION. Describe a time when you have been overwhelmed with the reality of darkness and evil that is present in our world. How did you find comfort?

Judah had turned away from the light into the dark—to mediums and spiritists, to ghosts that gibber and squeak (8:19-20). King Ahaz has turned away from the sign God offered him, but a greater King is coming to put things right. This king is a child rather than a mighty conqueror! Yet he has shoulders adequate to the task. He shares God's character as a Wonderful Counselor. He is described as Mighty God. Paradoxically, although a son, he is described as the Everlasting Father! He is Prince of Peace and his kingdom shares his character. He is a descendant of David and will rule his kingdom with justice and righteousness forever. All of these characteristics distinguish his kingdom from the chronic instability of Israel and the desperate wobbling of Judah. *Read Isaiah 8:19—9:17.*

1. Where are the Israelites looking for wisdom according to verses 8:19-20?

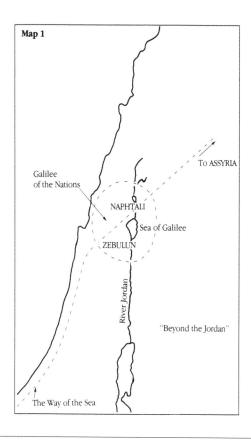

Map 1

Galilee
of the Nations

To ASSYRIA

NAPHTALI

Sea of Galilee

ZEBULUN

River Jordan

"Beyond the Jordan"

The Way of the Sea

2. The people are very distressed (8:21-22). Why do they curse their king and their God?

3. Find the regions of Zebulun, Naphtali and Galilee, and the road called "the Way of the Sea" on map 1. The Way of the Sea marked the western limits of Palestine, and the Jordan marked the eastern limits. What change from their present condition does Isaiah predict in 9:1-2?

4. How would you describe the connection between abandoning God's law and testimony (8:20) and society's spiritual darkness (8:22) from conditions today?

5. The light dawns in 9:2-5. What specific changes does Isaiah predict?

6. Amazing changes follow in society when the light dawns. What evidence is there in the Gospels of surprise, disbelief and contempt when he who was called "the Light of the world" began his work in Galilee?

7. The part of the world highlighted in 9:1 is one of the world's trouble spots today. Pause and pray for the different peoples whose homes were or are in this area.

8. Verses 2-5 are the trumpet fanfare announcing the arrival of a Gideon-like military hero (look at Judges 7:19-21). But what is the new arrival like according to 9:6-7?

9. When was the kingdom spoken of in 9:7 established?

10. In what ways is the coming of the kingdom of justice and right-eousness (9:7) good news for the poor, the needy and the oppressed?

How can we be involved in its coming?

11. Which of these titles—"Wonderful Counselor, Mighty God, Ever-lasting Father and Prince of Peace"—particularly describes God as you have known him during a time of difficulty?

Praise the King for his kingdom which has come, is coming and will come. The enthusiasm of the Almighty will make it happen (9:7)!

Now or Later

12. Read Isaiah 9:8—10:4. The shadow of God's hand upraised in judgment hangs over this passage (9:12, 17, 21; 10:4). For what specific sins?

13. *Read Isaiah 10:5-34.* What will Assyria, God's ax of judgment, do? What will happen to her eventually (vv. 15-19)?

Where does Assyria's army stand at the moment (vv. 28-32)?

14. Judgment is not the last word. What will the remnant do (vv. 20-23)?

6

A Hope to Live By

Isaiah 11—12

Faith. Hope. Love. Hope is one of the three cardinal virtues. It is essential. We need hope to live.

GROUP DISCUSSION. List all the different types of hope you can think of. Where does authentic Christian hope lie on this spectrum?

PERSONAL REFLECTION. How do you strengthen or reassert your hopefulness in hard times?

In the first ten chapters of Isaiah there is a remarkable alternation of the imagery of light and darkness: not good news without the bad news of humanity's sinfulness, but not the bad news without the good news of God's redeeming grace. The hope expressed here is not a blind and shallow optimism. It is not a "you have never had it so good" philosophy borne along on the crest of economic prosperity. Reading the whole of Isaiah 7—12 shows how difficult and depressing the days of Ahaz were in many respects. Yet these chapters hold out in both general and specific terms a thrilling hope for the future. *Read Isaiah 11—12.*

---

1. Summarize the character of the person described as the "Branch" in verses 11:2-5.

2. The Holy Spirit is described as having six specific qualities in 11:2. What are they?

3. Which of these qualities do you most want the Spirit to work in your life at this time? Why?

4. How do you respond to the phrase "delight in the fear of the LORD"?

What forms of fear might be appropriate before Almighty God?

5. What does 11:6-9 teach about the character of the kingdom of the One who is called the "Branch"?

6. Are the transformations described here to characterize the church now, the world or the new heavens and new earth?

7. Some have taken the promise of verse 9 as an incentive for missionary labor and expectancy. Today this particular prospect is often eclipsed by a more gloomy understanding of the world's future. What are the dangers in the extreme of either point of view?

8. How does the great homecoming spoken of in 11:10-16 spell out in detail what the prophecy of 11:9 predicts?

9. How are the Branch of 11:1 and the Root of 11:10 related?

In what way is the fulfillment of the messianic prophecy equally paradoxical?

10. What are the main themes of the song of thanksgiving in chapter 12?

11. Drawing water is a frequent daily task (12:3). How can you constantly refresh your hopefulness?

Memorize the words of 12:2 and turn them into a daily prayer of affirmation: "Yes, God you are my salvation: I will trust and not be afraid. You, LORD, are my strength and my song; you have been and always will be my salvation."

Now or Later

In chapter 10 Isaiah described Assyria as God's ax of judgment. This asserts God's sovereignty over history in general terms. In chapters 13-23, this is worked out in greater or lesser detail with reference to many surrounding nations. Read these chapters as an interlude between Isaiah's early predictions of judgment and Assyria's arrival in chapter 28.

7

Our Spoiled World

Isaiah 24

Life on this planet is filled with paradox. The airplane and nuclear fusion were two of the twentieth century's most striking inventions. Beneficial results have followed but so have Hiroshima and Chernobyl. We see the beauty of the creation and are moved to offer God wondering thanks. Yet in the same moment we can be aware of natural crisis or disaster, signs of increasing planetary stress, and plead with God to preserve the earth. How would God have us view our relationship to the world?

GROUP DISCUSSION. Is ecology just a field for freaks and romantics? Or is there an appropriate role for the believer regarding environmental issues? Talk honestly about your perspectives.

PERSONAL REFLECTION. What do you personally contribute to global stress? What can you do about it?

Read Isaiah 24.

---

1. Picture the devastation described by the verbs of verses 1, 3 and 4. Describe any such devastation that you have seen.

2. What reasons are given in verses 5 and 6 for the devastation described?

What do verses 21-22 add to your understanding of the forces behind the devastation?

3. How comprehensive is the judgment described (see v. 2)?

4. What is the mood of verses 4-13?

5. What is your personal reaction to the global hangover described in 1-13, and why do you think you have that reaction?

6. Where do you find a cause for hope in verses 4-13?

7. These verses presuppose a close connection between the earth itself, the land and its inhabitants. In what ways can you see the godlessness of humanity taking its toll on the physical world today?

8. How do you account for the fragment of singing that bursts out in verses 14-16, only to be abruptly silenced by Isaiah's cry of pain in the latter part of verse 16?

9. What additional aspects of God's judgment are revealed in verses 16-20?

10. Who or what is included in the judgment according to verses 21-23?

11. In what ways should Christians, who believe in God as Creator as well as Savior, have a special concern for our beautiful, fragile world? What can you specifically do about this?

Pray for environmental scientists, that we will see more clearly the meaning of our human covenant with the earth.

Now or Later

How might we achieve a more appropriate equilibrium between a conservative theology and a conservationist lifestyle?

8

Free at Last!

Isaiah 25

Free at last, free at last!
Thank God A'mighty,
We are free at last!

This song, with eloquent simplicity, expresses the pervasive hope of oppressed, exploited and downtrodden people. Extreme conditions bring out a person's inner qualities. Some flourish. Some survive. Some give up.

GROUP DISCUSSION. What has helped you to come through a desperate situation?

PERSONAL REFLECTION. Describe an experience you have had in driving rain, a snowstorm or some other natural disaster in which you knew that God was present with you.

In this chapter a song of praise arises phoenix-like from the shattered world we saw in chapter 24. We read of Israel's joy at the downfall of God's enemies, the end of death itself and God's final victory. Derek Kidner titles this chapter "the great liberation," subtitling the sections: "the end of tyranny" (vv. 1-5), "the end of darkness and death" (vv. 6-8) and "the end of pride" (vv. 9-12).* As we read of God's triumph, embed the teaching of this chapter in your heart so that you may be strong in times of trouble. *Read Isaiah 25.*

1. How is God's character described in verse 1?

_____

2. What repeated adjective reveals the main target of God's judgment in verses 2-5?

_____

3. With what vivid metaphors does Isaiah describe God's relationship to the poor and needy (vv. 4-5)?

_____

4. "He will swallow up death forever. The Sovereign LORD will wipe away the tears." Describe a situation of death or bereavement in which you have plumbed the depths of these promises, and any hindrances you experienced in doing so.

_____

5. What will God provide, and what will he do at his wonderful banquet (vv. 6-8)?

_____

6. When are you most able to identify with the delighted response of verse 9?

_____

7. To what trial this very day should you make a similar response?

8. By what inelegant picture does Isaiah describe Moab's undignified end (vv. 11-12)?

9. According to verses 10-12, what is the particular sin that characterized Moab?

10. Return to the scene of God's banquet in verses 6-8. How does this wonderful imagery transform your understanding of death for the believer?

11. What is the significance of the phrase "on this mountain," which is repeated three times in this chapter?

Pray or write your own song of praise to God for the "marvelous things" he has planned (v. 1) for your life.

Now or Later

Isaiah 26 and 27 contain three wonderful promises that deserve our notice and contemplation.

12. *Read Isaiah 26:1-4.* The call to lifelong commitment is based on the assertion of God's rocklike faithfulness. What experiences have you had of the "perfect peace" that is promised here to the one whose undeviating mindset is focused on the Lord?

13. *Read Isaiah 26:8.* What behavior would follow if the Lord's name and his renown were truly the deepest desire of our souls?

14. *Read Isaiah 27:12-13.* The image of harvest is common in the Bible. Here it is a matter of sifting and saving. But finally all will be safely gathered in. What incentive does this give to us to be patient and steadfast in our task of witness?

Read Isaiah 26:4 again and quiet your heart with the following meditation:

Be still and know that I am God.
Be still and know that I am.
Be still and know.
Be still.
Be.

*Derek Kidner, "Isaiah," in *New Bible Commentary,* ed. G. J. Wenham, J. A. Motyer, D. A. Carson and R. T. France (Downers Grove, Ill.: InterVarsity Press, 1994), p. 648.

9

Who Can
You Trust?

Isaiah 30:1-18

There are perhaps two common reactions by believers in a society which is beginning to disintegrate. One is pessimistic withdrawal; the other is frantic activism, to the left or to the right. Neither of these addresses fundamental, foundational issues.

GROUP DISCUSSION. What is the best contribution that people of faith can make to a society that is in the process of dissolution?

PERSONAL REFLECTION. What is the difference between faith and wishful thinking?

In Isaiah 24—27 the prophet's vision has risen significantly above the everyday details of his society and world to a larger and longer vision of God's purposes. But now he returns to the everyday political realities. There were apparently many in Judah who were not at all sure that the Lord would be able to protect Jerusalem. Meanwhile, Isaiah still hammers away at the same message he has been preaching all along: "Trust in the Lord at all times." Military alliances can do little to preserve a society that is already corroded and rotten within. *Read Isaiah 30:1-18.*

1. Why does God object to Judah's taking shelter under the shadow of Egypt (vv. 1-5)?

2. How do verses 6-7 emphasize the utter futility of seeking Egypt's help?

3. What moral direction might someone who wants to work in foreign affairs derive from this passage?

4. From verses 8-11 describe the Israelites' behavior.

5. How is the metaphor Isaiah uses to depict God's judgment particularly appropriate to their sin (vv. 12-14)?

6. From verses 10-11, how do you think Isaiah was regarded by the people?

Why do you think the people responded to him in this way?

7. Describe a time when it has been difficult for you to trust in God.

8. Describe a time when you have experienced the kind of contentment verse 15 promises.

9. How do verses 16-17 depict the price of unbelief?

10. Consider some particular trouble you are facing at this time. What steps do you need to take in order to trust that God will be gracious to those who wait for him, as verse 18 promises?

11. Isaiah's listeners would have nothing to do with his message of repentant rest and quiet trusting (v. 15). "Out of the way!" they said (and no doubt other things as well). How may we so hear these words of Isaiah that their fragrance lingers over our whole lives?

Sometimes prayers like "Lord, help me not to be so anxious, so nervous" are so focused on the anxiety and nervousness that we end up worse rather than better! To prevent this we should turn some scriptural promises into affirmations:

> *Lord, I turn quietly to you for salvation;*
> *Lord, I trust quietly in you for strength:*
> *For you are full of compassion and grace.*
> *I praise you.*

Now or Later

Chapters 31-33 are further oracles from the time of the Assyrian crisis. Just as chapters 24-27 left chapters 13-23 far behind, so the visions of judgment and salvation in chapters 34 and 35 leave the detailed historical situation of 28-33 far behind. Read chapter 35 against the dark background of chapter 34. Ponder the joy of the new exodus; the transformation of the desert; the way of holiness, which even fools cannot miss; and the pilgrims returning to Zion "crowned with never-fading gladness."

10

The Source of Confidence

Isaiah 36—37

Believers in God are often subjected to attacks. Sometimes these are brutal and roaring; sometimes they are subtle and insinuating. How do we prepare for such attacks without developing an unhealthy defensiveness?

GROUP DISCUSSION. Have you ever been intimidated by someone's ability to present an argument? Have you ever been frustrated by someone's ability to twist your words and distort the truth? How do you respond in such situations?

PERSONAL REFLECTION. Are you by nature a confident person or a tentative person? What would help you to develop a modest but definite confidence in what you believe?

The political situation that had been developing for years comes to a tremendous climax in Isaiah 36—39. These chapters coincide almost exactly (except for Hezekiah's prayer in 38:9-20) with 2 Kings 18—20. The Assyrian army is right outside the gates of Jerusalem, and the Assyrian general assaults King Hezekiah's peace delegation with rude cleverness. But Isaiah and Hezekiah remain confident in God in this supreme test and are able to respond with force and conviction to the blasphemous words they hear. *Read Isaiah 36.*

1. Use map 2 to get a picture of the situation described in 36:1-3. (You may remember that the place where the Assyrian commander stood in verse 2 is the same spot where Isaiah had confronted Ahaz years earlier [see 7:3].) How do you think the Judeans and King Hezekiah were feeling at this point?

2. How would you characterize the attitude of the Assyrian field commander from his speeches in chapter 36?

3. What contradictions between the Israelites' words and actions does the field commander note in verses 5-6?

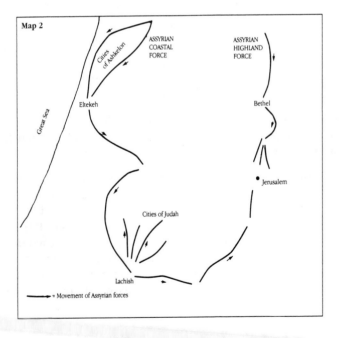

Map 2

ASSYRIAN COASTAL FORCE

ASSYRIAN HIGHLAND FORCE

Cities of Ashkelon

Great Sea

Eltekeh

Bethel

Jerusalem

Cities of Judah

Lachish

= Movement of Assyrian forces

4. Judah claimed to be relying on the Lord (36:7) but in practice had put a lot of effort into guaranteeing (they thought) Egypt's protection. How do you maintain a proper balance between "trusting the Lord" and "keeping your powder dry"?

5. How does the field commander distort the truth in verse 7 and in verse 10?

6. What temptations does the king of Assyria hold out in verses 16-20?

7. In what respects can you see parallels between the threats of the Assyrian general and the temptations you face?

8. How do the people and the court officials respond (vv. 21-22)?

9. *Read Isaiah 37:1-7.* What attitudes are demonstrated in Hezekiah's message to Isaiah and in Isaiah's reply?

10. Sennacherib's response (37:9-13) is a cruder replay of the threats of his field commander in chapter 36. *Read Isaiah 37:21-38.* What is the substance of Isaiah's reply to Sennacherib's taunt?

11. Contrast the word of hope to Hezekiah (37:30-32) and the shockingly brief statement about the end of Sennacherib's campaign and the end of his life (37:36-38).

12. In what respects can you take Hezekiah's and Isaiah's responses to Sennacherib as models for your own response to intimidation?

Pray that you will defend your faith with an appropriate boldness.

Now or Later

Isaiah 37:32 mentions the "zeal of the LORD almighty." This is a concept that deserves further study. What is the difference of meaning between *jealous* and *zealous*? What does the Bible mean when it describes God as a "jealous God"? It does not mean that he is self-centered and petty, or insecure, or frightened of losing respect! These things were features of the gods in some other religions. But God's jealousy is that of a faithful husband who will not share his wife's loyalty. He is jealous that we should not drink poison, thinking it to be wine. Thus Adrio Konig says, "Perhaps the best description of God's jealousy is that he is a God who *cares*" (Adrio König, *Here am I* [Grand Rapids, Mich.: Eerdmans, 1982], p. 95).

11

How Quick
We Are to Forget

Isaiah 38—39

A man described his problem of memory loss to a psychiatrist. "How long have you had this problem?" he was asked. "What problem?" he replied.

The humor is found in the idea that a person could forget so much so fast. And yet we may find ourselves suffering from a similar level of forgetfulness.

GROUP DISCUSSION. Have you had a remarkable experience that you thought would make a decisive difference to your life, only to find that old habits die hard and it is harder to remember than to forget?

PERSONAL REFLECTION. Which do you believe is more dangerous to an attitude of faith—adversity or prosperity? Why?

It was a miracle. Hezekiah's life was extended by fifteen years! We might expect that he would live those fifteen years in unforgettable gratitude and trustfulness, but the Bible, with its usual dogged realism, records that it was not so. In the chapter that follows we will see how Hezekiah ignored the warnings he had been given and invited a treacherous enemy into his home. *Read Isaiah 38.*

---

1. How do you reconcile the Lord's word in verse 1 that Hezekiah would not recover and his promise in verse 5 that Hezekiah would live fifteen more years?

2. What exactly was the sign God gave to Hezekiah (vv. 7-8)?

3. Have you had any amazing signs of God's goodness in answer to prayer? Describe them and indicate how permanent a mark they have made on your life.

4. With what vivid metaphors does Hezekiah describe his deathly sickness (vv. 10-14)?

5. From verse 18 what do you think Hezekiah understood about death?

6. What reassurance does Hezekiah find in God's love in verses 15-20?

7. What abiding truths do you find in chapter 38 to hold on to firmly in times of sickness and misfortune?

8. *Read Isaiah 39:1-8.* Derek Kidner has said of these verses, "The faith of Hezekiah, proof against the heaviest blows, melts at the touch of flattery . . . and the world claims another victim by its friendship" (Kidner, "Isaiah," p. 655). Do you think this is a fair assessment of 39:14? Why or why not?

9. What punishment did Isaiah announce for Hezekiah's disloyalty (39:5-7)?

10. How do you interpret Hezekiah's response—his words and his thoughts (39:8)?

11. In what ways does this passage expand or change your understanding of who God is and how he answers our prayers?

Pray for a sharper remembrance of all God's mercies, so that the life changes these enable may be deeper and more stable.

Now or Later

Cast your mind back over the first eleven studies in Isaiah. What incentives have these studies given you to trust in God through troubled times? Rehearse these lessons while things are well with you. When the exam time comes, the time for revision is over. When the hurricane arrives, it is too late to batten down the roof tiles.

12

A Hope That Never Tires

Isaiah 40

Throughout history, God the Holy One, God the Gracious One, unwearyingly speaks to his people, revealing himself as a God of grace, an incomparably great God, and a God who is in charge of the movements of history, even when a tyrant arises to terrify the world. The nations in terror turn to their idols.

GROUP DISCUSSION. Describe some situations in which you think people turn to idols (for instance, money, power or sex) as a source of comfort in times of difficulty or trouble.

PERSONAL REFLECTION. Call to mind a time when you experienced God's comfort in a very special way.

In Isaiah 40 and the chapters following, the ending of the Babylonian exile is presupposed, and it is the prophet's purpose to reconstruct his people's faith and hope with prophecies of liberation from captivity and a new calling to be God's servant and a light to the nations. In the whole mountain range of the Bible some of the highest and most wonderful peaks are to be found in these chapters. *Read Isaiah 40.*

---

1. A tender, wooing voice speaks to God's people in verses 1 and 2. What are the implications of the three affirmations all introduced by the word *that?*

2. The word *comfort* in the Bible has more in common with the words *fortress* and *fortitude* than with the word *comfortable*. Unpack the resilience and inner strength of this idea of comfort.

3. What sort of road is the herald calling for in verses 3-5?

4. Deserts, valleys and mountains are hindrances to transport and communication. If all people are to see the glory of the Lord, these obstacles must be removed. What obstacles do you and your small group or church face in both your local witness and global missions efforts?

How can these obstacles be removed?

5. A second voice is raised in verses 6-8. What vivid contrast is made in these verses?

6. A third voice, in verse 9, says, "Here is your God!" What sort of a God is he according to verses 10 and 11?

48 —————————————————————— *I s a i a h*

7. When have you known God's power, and when have you known his gentleness, as in verses 10-11?

8. In what different ways is the incomparable greatness of God affirmed by the avalanche of questions and statements in verses 12-17 and 21-26?

9. From the soaring vision of God in verses 12-17, Isaiah presents a sweeping critique of idolatry in verses 18-20. How does Isaiah's approach compare to the way in which we handle idolatry in the church today?

10. What results follow from the declaration that our God is in control of the stars (vv. 25-26)?

11. What is Israel's complaint in verse 27? How does the prophet answer (vv. 28-31)?

12. Notice the order of the words *soar, run, walk* in verse 31. What reasons can you suggest for the unusual order of these promises?

13. How do these verses bring you the encouragement you need today?

Praise God for his inexhaustible energy and unfathomable wisdom: a secure foundation for a hope that never tires.

Now or Later

The contrast between Almighty God and useless idols continues in chapter 41.

---

14. *Read Isaiah 41:1-7 and 21-29.* God is raising up a mighty world conqueror from the northeast (a reference to Cyrus the Medo-Persian). What is the people's panic-stricken response to this emergency?

---

15. *Read Isaiah 41:8-20.* What three images of comfort and encouragement strengthen Israel in these traumatic times?

Saturate your soul with the images of verses 17-20 until you arise refreshed and strong again.

13

"Here Is My Servant"

Isaiah 42

One of Jesus' most memorable sayings is found in Mark 10:45: "The Son of Man did not come to be served, but to serve, and to give his life as a ransom for many." One of Jesus' most memorable actions took place in the upper room where he was having his last meal with his disciples, and he washed their feet. Afterward he said, "You call me 'Teacher' and 'Lord,' and rightly so, for that is what I am. . . . I have set you an example that you should do as I have done for you" (John 13:13, 15).

GROUP DISCUSSION. Why is it so hard for people of importance to serve others? What hinders them?

PERSONAL REFLECTION. Write a thank-you note to someone who has thoughtfully and kindly served you in a difficult time.

The roots of these memorable words and deeds of our Lord are in these chapters of Isaiah, in which God reveals the character of the deliverer whom he is going to provide for Israel, a mighty deliverer who will yet be a lowly servant, speaking first of him and then to him. *Read Isaiah 42.*

---

1. What positive and negative phrases are used to describe God's servant in verses 1-4?

2. Now picture yourself as the servant. Are you conscious of God's *delight* resting upon you? Explain how you respond to this image.

---

3. In verses 5-9 God addresses his servant. What has God done and what will God do for the servant according to verses 5-9?

---

4. How would you summarize the servant's functions or duties according to verses 1-9?

---

5. What is the scope of the servant's ministry (vv. 4, 6)?

---

6. In what ways does the description of the servant and his ministry foreshadow our Lord's person and work?

---

7. In what respect or respects does this passage challenge you—your character, your service?

---

8. What vivid metaphors do verses 10-17 use to describe the Lord at work?

9. How do verses 18-25 describe the state of the people of Israel?

What is the explanation for their present condition?

---

10. Promises are needed because people are so often liars. But every word of God is a promise—what he says, he *will do.* Look in this chapter at the verbs that God is the subject of. Which one or ones can you take as a personal promise of God to you now?

This text tells us that the servant is gentle (v. 3) and yet is commissioned to bring justice, law and covenant to the earth. Praise God for the gentle, mighty Deliverer he has provided for us.

Now or Later

What is the difference between meekness and weakness?

How can you develop a strong gentleness?

14

You Are Precious

Isaiah 43:1—44:5

How do you feel when you hear the words "I love you"?

Many of us have never, or seldom, heard these words. And like a radio signal cluttered with static noise, the true meaning of the words is distorted by their overuse or misuse in countless songs, books and movies.

GROUP DISCUSSION. In a culture where many love words have been devalued, how can we revalue them? (Or even invent new words?)

PERSONAL REFLECTION. On what do you base your sense of self-worth?

In this passage we will hear the words "I love you" afresh so that we can be made abundantly sure of God's love for us personally. *Read Isaiah 43:1—44:5.*

1. The words "but now" in verse 1 introduce a contrast between 42:18-25 and 43:1-7. What is this contrast?

2. Pick out the verbs in 43:1-7 of which God is the subject and God's people (Israel and her descendants) are the object. How do you feel about being the object of such statements?

3. Isaiah 43:2 has provided encouragement for countless believers in times of trouble. Describe what you have experienced of God's presence through times of trouble.

---

4. Israel is called to an international assembly of idol worshipers and their idols in 43:8-13. To what does the Lord call her to witness?

---

5. The Jews' position appears to be hopeless. But according to 43:14-15, what is God going to do to Babylon?

---

6. What would the significance of 43:16-17 have been for the Israelites?

---

7. What is God going to do for Israel (43:19-21)?

---

8. We have been formed to praise God (43:21). We are "wired for praise." Do you only praise God when you feel like it? Or do you praise God in order to feel as you should?

---

9. Israel's slavish religiosity (43:23-24) does not please God. What promise does God repeat to his people (43:25)?

What warning does he give them (43:27-28)?

10. Isaiah 43:19 says "See, I am doing a new thing." What new thing do you need to look with expectant faith for God to do for you?

_____

11. Just as the "but now" of 43:1 shines brightly against the dark background of 42:18-25, the "but now" of 44:1 shines brightly against the dark background of 43:22-28. God's patience has not expired. What does he promise his people in 44:1-5?

_____

12. Visualize the homecoming of God's people (43:5-7) and the addition of foreigners to their numbers (44:5). How did it come about?

How will it come about?

Pray that the assurance of God's love, expressed in 43:4, will give you the strength to go through the trials described in 43:2.

Now or Later

Isaiah 44:9-20 is the high point of Isaiah's exposure of the emptiness of idolatry: a man cuts a piece of wood in half; one piece he uses as firewood, and the other piece he makes into a god. A person who does this, who trusts in things that they have made, has not stopped to think (44:19).

In contrast to this, burst into song to the wonderful Creator God, who has made everything and made you (44:24), who cancels sin (44:22), and who controls even the movements of superpowers (44:28). He is not too great to care for you; he is too great to fail you.

15

Turning to God

Isaiah 45

There is a well-known story of the conversion, on January 6, 1850, of the great Baptist preacher C. H. Spurgeon. One Sunday, while he was still a teenager, he attended a service at a primitive Methodist chapel. Because a snowstorm had prevented the appointed preacher from arriving, one of the stewards, a shoemaker, had to teach. Having nothing much to say, he stuck to the words of his text, Isaiah 45:22, which he repeated several times: "Turn to me and be saved, all you ends of the earth; for I am God, and there is no other." Finally, recognizing Spurgeon as a stranger, he said, "Young man, you look very miserable—look to Jesus. Look. Look. Look!"

"I looked," said Spurgeon, "until I could almost have looked my eyes away; and in heaven I will look still, in joy unutterable."

GROUP DISCUSSION. Isaiah 45:22 calls on the whole world to turn to God, the only God there is. What difficulties does this cause many people, including believers, in our pluralistic age?

PERSONAL REFLECTION. In what ways is it difficult for you to see the caring providence of God operating in your life and circumstances?

Verse 22 invites the whole world to turn to the Lord, for to him (and, as is later revealed, to Jesus) every knee will bow. The joy of receiving this invitation is to energize us play our part in its fulfillment. *Read Isaiah 45.*

1. In 44:23 God says of Cyrus (king of Babylon) that he is his shepherd who will cause Jerusalem and the temple to be rebuilt. What will God do for Cyrus according to 45:1-8?

---

2. Verse 4 and verse 6 introduce at least two reasons that God will use Cyrus. What are these reasons?

---

3. What practical conclusions follow from the statements of this chapter that behind the activities of a world conqueror (v. 1), behind darkness as well as light (v. 7), behind disaster as well as prosperity (v. 7) stands the sovereign Lord God?

---

4. Have there been times when you complained about or to God? How did God reply?

---

5. In verses 9-13, why does Israel complain, and what is God's reply?

---

6. Why do you think Isaiah's rebuke (vv. 9-10) and God's reminder (v. 11) came to Israel in this way?

---

7. In verse 14 the Lord speaks to Israel. In verses 15-17 Isaiah marvels at the amazing ways of God. In verses 18-19 the Lord speaks. How are the foreigners who come to Israel described (v. 14)?

8. What do verses 14-19 say about God's relationship with Israel?

---

9. In verses 20-25 the horizons widen to the "ends of the earth." What are these foreigners summoned to do?

---

10. What is the implication of the phrase "by myself I have sworn" in verse 23?

---

11. In Romans 14:11 how does Paul apply verse 23 to our Lord Jesus Christ?

What are the implications of this verse for our lives?

Praise God for his wonderful, overarching providence over all the circumstances of your life, and pray for any friends or relatives who have not yet turned to him.

Now or Later

> "Thy wonderful, grand will, my God
> holds fast in its divine embrace
> my captive will, a gladsome bird,
> prisoned in such a realm of grace."

An eagle is free to fly through the air; a whale's freedom lies in the ocean, and our freedom lies in glad submission to God's will. Are you more and more confident that this is indeed the case? Talk honestly with God about ways in which you struggle with trust.

16

Strong Foundations for Service

Isaiah 49:1-18

Some lonely, sick people give up and die. Others, equally ill, who receive visits and support from friends and family, recover. The mind and body are intricately connected.

GROUP DISCUSSION. What are the characteristics of an encourager? Why is encouragement so important?

PERSONAL REFLECTION. When depression, discouragement or despair comes your way, how do you deal with it?

Isaiah 42:1-25 was the first passage in which the Lord began to reveal to Isaiah the character of the mighty Deliverer he was going to send, who would yet be a lowly servant. This passage is the second so-called servant song that reveals more about the servant and what he will be like. The words apply preeminently to our Lord, but all his servants can take them too as a pattern for their ministry. *Read Isaiah 49:1-18.*

---

1. In verses 1-3 the servant of the Lord describes the Lord's call. What phrases in these verses describe the Lord's comprehensive preparation of his servant?

2. Trace in the history and geography and genealogy of your own life the loving foreknowledge of God. How has God prepared you for important events and opportunities to serve?

How does this strengthen your sense of God's calling?

3. How does the servant correct his first despairing response (v. 4) to the Lord's call?

4. The Lord gives the servant a wider commission in verses 5-7. What is this wider commission, and what will be its result?

5. How do the servant's reactions to the Lord's call in verses 1-7 encourage us in our own attempts to serve God?

6. The Lord is going to save his people, and the servant is going to be the mediator of his covenant with the people. How do verses 8-12 describe different aspects of God's salvation?

7. In what ways do verses 8-12 give a foretaste of the ministry of Jesus Christ?

8. What is the full meaning of "comforts" and "will have compassion" in verse 13?

Why is this a reason for the universe to start singing?

---

9. Israel (Zion) responds with a complaint—not a song—in verse 14. By what arguments does the Lord refute the complaint in verses 15-18?

---

10. Review the forces marshaled in this passage for the battle against discouragement and despair. How does this knowledge help you with the daily battles you face?

---

11. Read verses 1 and 6 again, and reflect on the servant's far-reaching international ministry. Think too of how the risen Lord gave his universal commission (Matthew 28:16-20) to a group of runaways. How may we keep this global perspective in our hearts?

Use this meditation to renew your delighted obedience to the one "whose service is perfect freedom":
That you are Lord to me—suffices me for strength;
That I am servant to you—suffices me for glory.

Now or Later
Draw a story line of your life. Mark four of the peaks when you have been full of confidence and peace and joy. Mark four of the troughs when life was hard and dark. Note the trend of the story. What hope does the study you have just done give you for the future trajectory of the line you have drawn?

17

The Burning Heart of Scripture

Isaiah 52:13—53:12

Devotion. A starving mother literally gives herself to the child she nurses. Self-sacrifice. Maximilian Kolbe, a Catholic priest, takes the place of a family man in the punishment cell of a Nazi concentration camp and starves to death.

GROUP DISCUSSION. What is it about stories like the ones above that moves us?

PERSONAL REFLECTION. Think of a time when someone has suffered for you. Describe what you think the experience of suffering was like.

There is a rising tide of expectancy and excitement in Isaiah 51—52 as the time for the Jews' release from captivity draws nearer. Isaiah 51:9-11 records a prayer for God to act and pictures the exiles coming home to Zion "crowned with never-fading gladness." Then, in 52:1 Jerusalem is told to awake and arise from the dust. Why? A runner is approaching over the mountains with good news: God is about to deliver his people. It is time to leave Babylon.

In this passage we are introduced again to the servant of the Lord, whose solitary agony is the price of his people's homecoming. *Read Isaiah 52:13—53:12.*

1. What reaction do many people have to the servant? Why (52:14-15)?

2. What will happen to the servant—and to the nations (52:13)?

3. In 52:10 we are told that the Lord is going to "lay bare his holy arm," that is, "roll up his sleeves" to save his people. But when he does so, what sort of person is revealed (53:1-3)?

4. How do these verses 4-6 explain the servant's sufferings?

5. How did the servant conduct himself in the midst of his suffering (53:7-9), and what was the result?

6. What will be the sequel to and the result of the servant's suffering (53:10-12)?

7. What, for you, are the most striking ties between this prophecy and the experiences of Jesus Christ our Lord?

8. Compare 1 Peter 2:21-25 to Isaiah 53. What are the parallels?

9. Why do you think Peter drew on Isaiah 52—53 in his letter?

10. Suggest reasons why 53:5 is called the "burning heart" of the Old Testament and indeed of the whole Bible.

11. How do you respond to this graphic description of how Christ suffered for you?

Express your worship and gratitude to the One who loved us and gave himself for us.

Now or Later

The hymn writer Isaac Watts (1674-1748) wrote one of the most famous hymns about the cross: "When I Survey the Wondrous Cross." He also wrote a lesser-known but even more profound hymn on the subject, "Nature with Open Volume Stands." Write in your own words a response to verses 3 and 4 of this six-verse hymn:

Here [at the cross] His whole name appears complete:
Nor wit can guess, nor reason prove,
Which of the letters best is writ,
The power, the wisdom or the love.

Here I behold His inmost heart,
Where grace and vengeance strangely join,
Piercing His Son with sharpest smart,
To make the purchased pleasures mine.

18

Shout for Joy

Isaiah 54—55

On May 30, 1792, at the Friar Lane Meeting House, Nottingham, England, William Carey preached an impassioned sermon on Isaiah 54:2-3 to a small group of local Baptist ministers. He rammed his sermon home with a pair of phrases that have been ringing ever since: "Expect great things from God; attempt great things for God." On October 2 he followed up his appeal, and these village pastors started the Particular Baptist Society for the Propagation of the Gospel Among the Heathen (later shortened to the Baptist Missionary Society).

GROUP DISCUSSION. Bishop Lesslie Newbigin, when he was eighty-eight years old, once began a talk with the words, "Mission begins with an explosion of joy!" Explain what this might mean and how it might be so.

PERSONAL REFLECTION. Describe a time when you have been overcome with the joy of knowing God in the midst of sorrow.

In this study the expectancy which has been heightening through previous chapters explodes into song and exhortation. A visitor to a harp shop observed that when the strings of the largest harp were plucked, all the other harps in the shop rang in unison with them. Let your heart vibrate to Isaiah's music in this study. *Read Isaiah 54.*

---

1. Isaiah 54:1-10 is an extended, complex metaphor applied to the relationship between Jerusalem and the Lord. What is the metaphor?

2. What has happened to Zion, and what will happen to her?

---

3. Tell what you know of God's "deep compassion," "everlasting kindness," "everlasting love" and wonderful "compassion." How much have you drawn on this fathomless bank account of grace?

---

4. In Isaiah 54:11-17 the metaphor changes to that of a rebuilt city. What will characterize this city?

---

5. Is the fulfillment of these marvelous promises to Jerusalem in the past, present or future?

---

6. God's love for you is more unshakable than the mountains (the ancient world's most immovable objects, 54:10). What are the implications of this statement for your life now?

---

7. *Read Isaiah 55.* An amazing offer is extended in 55:1-5. Who is invited, and what are they invited to?

---

8. A note of urgency is introduced in 55:6-7. How do these verses outline the nature of true repentance?

9. What transformations do God's thoughts and words achieve according to 55:8-13?

10. Here again is the place where the eternal word of God intersects with our lives today. Is there some way in which you need to seek the Lord (55:6), again or for the first time, for abundant life and for free pardon?

11. In what place or situation do you need to "go out in joy and be led forth in peace" and see transformations that today may seem impossible?

Turn away from your problems and joys to worship the Lord for who he is, as revealed in these chapters, quite apart from what he has particularly done for you. We need to recollect sometimes the wonder that God is, and not just what he is.

Now or Later

Reflect on a particularly joyful person whom you know or on a particularly joy-full season of your life. What were the deepest roots of the joy that you saw or experienced? How do joy and peace, both gifts of grace (not our anxious achievements), coexist and counterpoint in your own life? How can they become more deeply rooted?

19

Jeans of Joy & Shirts of Praise

Isaiah 61

On April 3, 1739, following George Whitefield's example, John Wesley preached for the first time in the open air, in Bristol, England, using Isaiah 61:1-2 as his text. He wrote about it, "I could scarce reconcile myself at first to this strange way of preaching in the fields; having been all my life, till very lately, so tenacious of every point relating to decency and order, that I should have thought the saving of souls almost a sin if it had not been done in a church." Thus began a ministry of over fifty years of outdoor preaching.

GROUP DISCUSSION. What are the different paths by which people come out of grief? Why do some people seem much more resilient than others?

PERSONAL REFLECTION. Think of a time you felt like an outcast. Who or what brought you comfort?

When Jerusalem was destroyed, some people contemptuously nicknamed it "Zion for whom no one cares" (Jeremiah 30:17). Jerusalem was utterly despised and alone. But God can delete the indelible and heal the incurable. In this chapter we see his healing and restorative work through his servant. The healing depicted here is as long as time and as wide as the created world, and we can have a part in it as well. *Read Isaiah 61.*

1. Jesus inaugurated his public ministry with verses 1 and 2 at Nazareth (Luke 4:16-21). Imagine you were to give a message based on these verses. What would you say?

2. Summarize the transforming ministry of the Lord's anointed servant in verses 1-3.

3. What metaphors are used in verse 3?

What kind of image does each one give you?

4. How do these verses help provide encouragement in areas of personal need?

5. Those who God transforms are to live lives which "display his beauty" (v. 3). What implications does this statement carry for our witness?

6. How do verses 4-9 depict Zion's transformed situation?

7. What will the reaction of Zion's people be?

8. How could the predictions of verses 4-9 be understood metaphorically (referring to nations outside Israel)?

9. How are the two metaphors for righteousness found in the delighted outburst of song in verses 10-11 appropriate?

10. There is a strong emphasis in this chapter on "righteousness" (vv. 3, 10-11) and "justice" (v. 8). How can you take a stand for justice this week for the glory of God's name?

11. This chapter speaks of everlasting joy (v. 7). What is the secret of a joy that never fades?

Pray for the poor, for the brokenhearted and for prisoners.

Now or Later

The year 1763 was a year of great revival in Wales under Howel Harris. Daniel Rowlands found himself compelled to defend English objections to the physical and spiritual joy of the people: "You English blame us, the Welsh, and speak against us and say, 'Jumpers! Jumpers!' But we Welsh have something also to allege against you and we most justly say of you, 'Sleepers!' 'Sleepers!'" (John Owen, *Memoir of Daniel Rowlands* [London, 1840], pp. 85ff.). As you reflect on your own life and that of your church or Christian group, which charge is most likely to stick?

What steps can you take toward a life more filled with praise?

20

The Exhilaration
of God's Love

Isaiah 62

Have you ever wondered what it is like to be a refugee? Have you ever wondered how it feels to pick up the few belongings you can carry and with a sick heart to leave your family home, your family farm, your family graves, your town, your country—perhaps never to return? But what if the chance comes to return home, for a new start under a new regime?

GROUP DISCUSSION. At the beginning of a new millennium there are over ninety million people living outside their countries as immigrants or as refugees. Why do you think this is, and what feelings do you think these people have?

PERSONAL REFLECTION. What is the meaning of your name? Do you know the motives of the ones who gave it to you?

The exultation and bridal joyousness of this chapter must be understood from the perspective of the returning refugees. The Judeans might have thought that Jerusalem had been irreversibly abandoned by the Lord—but it is not so. *Read Isaiah 62.*

1. What for you is the most joyful thing about a wedding day?

2. Isaiah has not kept silent about Judah's wickedness and its judgment. What motive does verse 1 reveal about Israel's refusal to keep silent?

3. How do verses 2-5 describe the new relationship between God and Zion?

4. Who are the "they" of verse 4?

5. Pause and dwell on Zion's new names. Hephzibah means "my delight is in her," and Beulah means "married." How do you respond to these names as expressions of God's feelings toward you as one of his people?

6. What will the role of Jerusalem's watchmen be?

7. What is promised in verses 8-9?

8. Describe the scene that verse 10 sets up.

---

9. What role do celebratory processions and marches of witness have in the church today?

---

10. What is the reward and recompense that will accompany the Lord (v. 11)?

---

11. Respond in joyful prayer and worship to the God who calls you "Sought After, the City No Longer Deserted" (v. 12).

Pray for any you know who are far from God, and for any who are far from home.

Now or Later

The solitary Avenger of 63:1-6 is a similar figure to that of 59:15-21. It is an awe-inspiring reminder of the "day of vengeance" mentioned in 61:2 and developed in even more titanic terms in Revelation 19:11-16. There are no victories, no liberations without cost. But even in this passage the dominant interest is in the One who is "mighty to save." Read this passage as a background to what follows.

21

A Cry for
Forgiveness & Revival

Isaiah 63:7—64:12

Have you ever been discouraged when you look at the people of God as they are today? Do you compare your church members to what they have been at various times in the past? Do you feel inadequate to the golden vision of what the church will be when Christ presents to God "a radiant church, without stain or wrinkle or any other blemish, but holy and blameless" (Ephesians 5:27)?

GROUP DISCUSSION. Revivals are remarkable, widespread turnings to God. Do you feel that we need a revival in the church today? Explain your response.

PERSONAL REFLECTION. Have you personally had any very striking, fresh experiences of God? What preceded them?

It is a shattering experience for Isaiah to turn from the vision of radiant Zion in 60—62 to Zion as it is. *Read Isaiah 63:7-19.*

1. What do we learn from the way that Isaiah begins his long and passionate prayer in verse 7?

2. Verse 9 recalls how God brought his people out of slavery in Egypt. How do verses 8-9 describe the warmth of God's relationship with his people?

3. Why should prayer always be framed in praise and thanks?

4. What was God's reaction to Israel's rebellion, according to verse 10?

5. What do the chastened people remember about God's wonderful deeds (vv. 11-14)?

6. Isaiah's review of God's actions speaks of God as Savior and as enemy in close proximity (63:8, 10). Why do these descriptions seem inconsistent, and even contradictory, to many modern readers?

7. Are there two sides to God's character, to either of which we may be arbitrarily subject?

8. *Read Isaiah 64:1-12.* What striking phrase, repeated three times in 63:16—64:12, gives the prayer its special intensity (63:16; 64:8)?

9. What diagnosis of Israel's condition does Isaiah's prayer disclose?

10. How does Isaiah see God's hand in this sorry state of affairs, and how does Israel look to God to get them out of it (63:15, 17; 64:1, 4-5, 8)?

11. God's interventions are always surprising. How do you see God intervening in the world today?

12. How can following the model of this passage enrich and deepen your own prayer life?

Pray that God will bring revival to you, your church and your nation.

Now or Later

Chapter 64 ends with a question in verse 12. It is by no means certain that Isaiah's people share his passionate contrition. *Read Isaiah 65:1-16,* and notice how unsparingly Isaiah sharpens the contrast between light and darkness: those who continue to provoke the Lord will feel his judgment again, but for those whom he recognizes as his servants there will be joys which cause all past troubles to be forgotten.

Read Romans 10:10-21 for another example of the miracle of divine restraint toward a stubborn and rebellious people. What does Almighty God do? He holds out his hands . . . all day long. Finally, as we know, he stretched out his hands on the cross. It is the utmost the mercy can do for the impenitent. How do you respond to the God who extends his hands to you?

22

The Terror &
the Glory

Isaiah 65:17—66:24

Hope has a life-preserving character. Time and again, as prison-camp memoirs show, people who have something to live for survive, and those who lose hope die under the same conditions.

GROUP DISCUSSION. Hope can be wishful thinking; it can be based on unreality. What are the dimensions (or characteristics) of true hope?

PERSONAL REFLECTION. Do you think it is possible to have perfectly righteous anger (with no false motives)?

All through Isaiah, the basic theme has been that God's faithful love should be the basis of his people's faithful trust. Now, as he brings his book to a climax, he describes the day when faith and hope will come to fruition. There will be a new heaven and a new earth in which love reigns. Yet this is not a fairy-tale ending. As in chapter 6, Isaiah cannot avert his eyes from the fact that some people reject the good news. One day their refusal will be irreversibly confirmed. *Read Isaiah 65:17-25.*

---

1. What simple joys and pleasures characterize the new heavens and new earth (65:17-19, 24)?

2. Why do you think the hopes of verses 17-25 are expressed in such down-to-earth fashion?

Does this meet your expectations? Why or why not?

3. How do you picture the new heavens and the new earth?

4. "Before they call I will answer" (v. 24). How has this been true in your life?

5. *Read Isaiah 66:1-24.* What is God's complaint (66:1-2)?

6. What worshipers does God esteem (66:2)? What worshipers displease God (66:3-4)?

7. How may we best preserve the two poles of awe and intimacy that characterize true worship?

8. According to 66:7-11, the apparently barren, abandoned and childless Zion is to have children. What aspects of the childbirth metaphor are stressed here?

9. One day God will finally show his hand (66:14) and gather all the nations together for a final demonstration of his power and glory. What are the negative aspects of this last intervention (66:14-16, 24)?

10. When this chapter is read in the synagogue, it is customary to read 66:23 again after 66:24. What are the positive aspects of God's final revelation of his glory (66:12-13, 19-23)?

11. To conclude your study in Isaiah, read or sing the following, and describe how the hope it expresses encourages you to trust God.

O the joy to see Thee reigning,
Thee, my own beloved Lord!
Every tongue Thy Name confessing,
Worship, honor, glory, blessing
Brought to Thee with glad accord;
Thee, my Master and my Friend,
Vindicated and enthroned,
Unto earth's remotest end
Glorified, adored and owned.
(F. R. Havergal, "Thou Art Coming, O My Saviour")

Praise God for the ways in which this series of studies has strengthened your faith so that you will be able to go on trusting him through thick and thin.

Now or Later

Ponder the following thought:

> I can imagine someone saying that he dislikes my idea of heaven as a place where we are patted on the back. But proud misunderstanding is behind that dislike. In the end that Face which is the delight or terror of the universe must be turned upon each of us either with one expression or with the other, either conferring glory inexpressible or inflicting shame that can never be cured or disguised. . . . It is written that we shall "stand before" Him, shall appear, shall be inspected. The promise of glory is the promise, almost incredible, and only possible by the work of Christ, that some of us, that any of us who really chooses, shall actually survive that examination, shall find approval, shall please God. To please God . . . to be a real ingredient in the divine happiness . . . to be loved by God, not merely pitied, but delighted in as an artist delights in his work or a father in a son—it seems impossible, a weight or burden of glory which our thoughts can hardly sustain. But so it is. (C S. Lewis, *The Weight of Glory and Other Addresses* [Grand Rapids, Mich.: Eerdmans, 1965], p. 10)

Leader's Notes

MY GRACE IS SUFFICIENT FOR YOU. (2 COR 12:9)

Leading a Bible discussion can be an enjoyable and rewarding experience. But it can also be *scary*—especially if you've never done it before. If this is your feeling, you're in good company. When God asked Moses to lead the Israelites out of Egypt, he replied, "O Lord, please send someone else to do it"! (Ex 4:13). It was the same with Solomon, Jeremiah and Timothy, but God helped these people in spite of their weaknesses, and he will help you as well.

You don't need to be an expert on the Bible or a trained teacher to lead a Bible discussion. The idea behind these inductive studies is that the leader guides group members to discover for themselves what the Bible has to say. This method of learning will allow group members to remember much more of what is said than a lecture would.

These studies are designed to be led easily. As a matter of fact, the flow of questions through the passage from observation to interpretation to application is so natural that you may feel that the studies lead themselves. This study guide is also flexible. You can use it with a variety of groups—student, professional, neighborhood or church groups. Each study takes forty-five to sixty minutes in a group setting.

There are some important facts to know about group dynamics and encouraging discussion. The suggestions listed below should enable you to effectively and enjoyably fulfill your role as leader.

Preparing for the Study

1. Ask God to help you understand and apply the passage in your own life. Unless this happens, you will not be prepared to lead others. Pray too for the various members of the group. Ask God to open your hearts to the message of his Word and motivate you to action.

2. Read the introduction to the entire guide to get an overview of the entire book and the issues which will be explored.

3. As you begin each study, read and reread the assigned Bible passage to familiarize yourself with it.

4. This study guide is based on the New International Version of the Bible. It will help you and the group if you use this translation as the basis for your

study and discussion.

5. Carefully work through each question in the study. Spend time in meditation and reflection as you consider how to respond.

6. Write your thoughts and responses in the space provided in the study guide. This will help you to express your understanding of the passage clearly.

7. It might help to have a Bible dictionary handy. Use it to look up any unfamiliar words, names or places. (For additional help on how to study a passage, see chapter five of *Leading Bible Discussions*, InterVarsity Press.)

8. Consider how you can apply the Scripture to your life. Remember that the group will follow your lead in responding to the studies. They will not go any deeper than you do.

9. Once you have finished your own study of the passage, familiarize yourself with the leader's notes for the study you are leading. These are designed to help you in several ways. First, they tell you the purpose the study guide author had in mind when writing the study. Take time to think through how the study questions work together to accomplish that purpose. Second, the notes provide you with additional background information or suggestions on group dynamics for various questions. This information can be useful when people have difficulty understanding or answering a question. Third, the leader's notes can alert you to potential problems you may encounter during the study.

10. If you wish to remind yourself of anything mentioned in the leader's notes, make a note to yourself below that question in the study.

Leading the Study

1. Begin the study on time. Open with prayer, asking God to help the group to understand and apply the passage.

2. Be sure that everyone in your group has a study guide. Encourage the group to prepare beforehand for each discussion by reading the introduction to the guide and by working through the questions in the study.

3. At the beginning of your first time together, explain that these studies are meant to be discussions, not lectures. Encourage the members of the group to participate. However, do not put pressure on those who may be hesitant to speak during the first few sessions. You may want to suggest the following guidelines to your group.

☐ Stick to the topic being discussed.

☐ Your responses should be based on the verses which are the focus of the discussion and not on outside authorities such as commentaries or speakers.

☐ These studies focus on a particular passage of Scripture. Only rarely should you refer to other portions of the Bible. This allows for everyone to participate in in-depth study on equal ground.

⎯ Anything said in the group is considered confidential and will not be discussed outside the group unless specific permission is given to do so.

⎯ We will listen attentively to each other and provide time for each person present to talk.

⎯ We will pray for each other.

4. Have a group member read the introduction at the beginning of the discussion.

5. Every session begins with a group discussion question. The question or activity is meant to be used before the passage is read. The question introduces the theme of the study and encourages group members to begin to open up. Encourage as many members as possible to participate, and be ready to get the discussion going with your own response.

This section is designed to reveal where our thoughts or feelings need to be transformed by Scripture. That is why it is especially important not to read the passage before the discussion question is asked. The passage will tend to color the honest reactions people would otherwise give because they are, of course, supposed to think the way the Bible does.

You may want to supplement the group discussion question with an ice-breaker to help people to get comfortable. See the community section of *Small Group Idea Book* for more ideas.

You also might want to use the personal reflection question with your group. Either allow a time of silence for people to respond individually or discuss it together.

6. Have a group member (or members if the passage is long) read aloud the passage to be studied. Then give people several minutes to read the passage again silently so that they can take it all in.

7. Question 1 will generally be an overview question designed to briefly survey the passage. Encourage the group to look at the whole passage, but try to avoid getting sidetracked by questions or issues that will be addressed later in the study.

8. As you ask the questions, keep in mind that they are designed to be used just as they are written. You may simply read them aloud. Or you may prefer to express them in your own words.

There may be times when it is appropriate to deviate from the study guide. For example, a question may have already been answered. If so, move on to the next question. Or someone may raise an important question not covered in the guide. Take time to discuss it, but try to keep the group from going off on tangents.

9. Avoid answering your own questions. If necessary, repeat or rephrase them until they are clearly understood. Or point out something you read in the leader's notes to clarify the context or meaning. An eager group quickly becomes passive and silent if they think the leader will do most of the talking.

10. Don't be afraid of silence. People may need time to think about the question before formulating their answers.

11. Don't be content with just one answer. Ask, "What do the rest of you think?" or "Anything else?" until several people have given answers to the question.

12. Acknowledge all contributions. Try to be affirming whenever possible. Never reject an answer. If it is clearly off-base, ask, "Which verse led you to that conclusion?" or again, "What do the rest of you think?"

13. Don't expect every answer to be addressed to you, even though this will probably happen at first. As group members become more at ease, they will begin to truly interact with each other. This is one sign of healthy discussion.

14. Don't be afraid of controversy. It can be very stimulating. If you don't resolve an issue completely, don't be frustrated. Move on and keep it in mind for later. A subsequent study may solve the problem.

15. Periodically summarize what the group has said about the passage. This helps to draw together the various ideas mentioned and gives continuity to the study. But don't preach.

16. At the end of the Bible discussion you may want to allow group members a time of quiet to work on an idea under "Now or Later." Then discuss what you experienced. Or you may want to encourage group members to work on these ideas between meetings. Give an opportunity during the session for people to talk about what they are learning.

17. Conclude your time together with conversational prayer, adapting the prayer suggestion at the end of the study to your group. Ask for God's help in following through on the commitments you've made.

18. End on time.

Many more suggestions and helps are found in *Leading Bible Discussions*, which is part of the LifeGuide Bible Study series.

Components of Small Groups

A healthy small group should do more than study the Bible. There are four components to consider as you structure your time together.

Nurture. Small groups help us to grow in our knowledge and love of God. Bible study is the key to making this happen and is the foundation of your small group.

Community. Small groups are a great place to develop deep friendships with other Christians. Allow time for informal interaction before and after each study. Plan activities and games that will help you get to know each other. Spend time having fun together—going on a picnic or cooking dinner together.

Worship and prayer. Your study will be enhanced by spending time praising

God together in prayer or song. Pray for each other's needs—and keep track of how God is answering prayer in your group. Ask God to help you to apply what you are learning in your study.

Outreach. Reaching out to others can be a practical way of applying what you are learning, and it will keep your group from becoming self-focused. Host a series of evangelistic discussions for your friends or neighbors. Clean up the yard of an elderly friend. Serve at a soup kitchen together, or spend a day working on a Habitat house.

Many more suggestions and helps in each of these areas are found in *Small Group Idea Book.* Information on building a small group can be found in *Small Group Leaders' Handbook* and *The Big Book on Small Groups* (both from InterVarsity Press). Reading through one of these books would be worth your time.

Study 1. Isaiah 1. No More Rotten Religion!
Purpose: To answer the questions "What sort of religiosity does God find empty and nauseating?" and "Into what relationship does he invite us?"

Question 1. The first metaphor is that of rebellious children. The second contrasts the nation's conduct unfavorably with that of domestic animals who know what to do.

Question 2. These verses give a kaleidoscopic picture of sinfulness. We read of a burden of guilt (v. 4), inherited corruption (v. 4), contemptuous spurning of the Lord and his will (v. 4), a sick and wounded society full of bruises and festering sores yet asking for more punishment (vv. 5-6)—like heroin addicts who head fatefully back to the drug that will kill them. The countryside is described as "desolate," "burned" and raped. The city of Jerusalem, God's own jewel, is compared to a crazy, forlorn shack in a melon field and to Sodom and Gomorrah—cities proverbial for their corruption and their obliteration by God's anger (Gen 18:16—19:26).

Question 4. The people were busy with their religion: sacrifices, offerings, incense, assemblies, weekly (sabbath) and monthly (new moon) festivals and ritualistic prayer. But God detests immoral religiosity; he finds their offerings meaningless. He wants to neither look nor listen. He cannot bear it.

Question 5. As with music approaching a climax, here a staccato effect is used by the prophet for emphasis. Note how short and sharp God's imperatives are here, contrasted with the measured pace of the invitation which follows.

Question 7. The virgin Jerusalem has become an unfaithful whore. Once she was full of righteousness but now she is full of murderers, impure silver, diluted wine and rulers who are corrupt crooks. So God intends to intervene with his purifying judgment.

Question 8. God's judgment is burning (v. 25), purging (v. 25), consuming

(v. 28), withering (v. 30), parching (v. 30), blazing (31). It will fall on unrepentant sinners. But God's purpose is not just destructive. A faith-full city is to be reconstructed, full of justice and righteousness.

Question 9. Some scholars think a gracious promise and invitation are inappropriate in this context. But the dual options of verses 19 and 20 almost require that verse 18 should be in the nature of a summary. Repentance is here presented as a rational confrontation with God. Scarlet and crimson were strong and bright colors. We must wash ourselves (v. 16), but only God's grace can "delete the indelible" (Derek Kidner in *New Bible Commentary*, ed. D. Guthrie and J. A. Motyer [Downers Grove, Ill.: InterVarsity Press, 1970], p. 634).

Study 2. Isaiah 2. Longing & Living for *That Day*.

Purpose: To study the characteristics of God's coming day of reckoning in order that we may long more deeply and live more simply toward that day.

Group discussion. The words quoted in the introduction still seem infinitely far from fulfillment. Globally, so-called defense spending exceeds the income of the poorest half of the world's population. Countries where citizens are starving spend millions on armaments. Draw out your group members' thoughts and ideas about the state of the world.

Question 1. The idea of the "day of the Lord," "that day" and "the last day" is quite prominent in the prophets. If the question arises, "To what period do these phrases refer?" it may be helpful to use the diagram below for explanation:

View A   *View B*

In view A the two circles or discs appear to be in the same plane. Only view B, a side view, shows that there is a separation depth-wise between them. So in prophecy, sometimes the prophets speak of various events with no apparent separation between different times of fulfillment. Only subsequently does it appear that the fulfillments take place at different times.

It looks as if the final fulfillment of these words in Isaiah lies still in the future, especially in the day of judgment. But we have already seen something of God's splendor, his righteousness, justice, salvation and his word going out through Jesus Christ and through his body, the church.

Question 2. From Psalm 68:15-18 it is clear that the preeminence of Jerusalem on its mountain, Mount Zion, is due to the fact that the temple is there, the place where God has placed his name, the symbol of his presence with his people.

Question 3. The nations come to worship God, to hear his Word, to learn his Law (or instruction), to find his ways and walk in his paths. They come for him to settle their disputes in a spirit of peace and joy. There is a delightful balance in this verse between knowledge and action.

Isaiah pictures the nations flowing in toward Jerusalem. Jesus, in Acts 1:8, speaks of the disciples spreading out to the ends of the earth. The images are complementary. Isaiah's vision is not ethnocentric, and Jesus anticipated the inflow of Gentiles into the church.

Question 6. The land is full of foreign superstitions (v. 6), clever alliances (v. 6), endless wealth (v. 7), military equipment (v. 7) and idols (v. 8). But "thronged though it is, the land is destitute: it has everything but God (6a)" (Kidner, "Isaiah," p. 635). Isaiah shouts for his compatriots to see the emptiness of the land—the emptiness of abandonment by God (v. 6) without forgiveness (v. 9).

Question 7. Nature's lofty things are mentioned: Lebanon cedars (now very rare), Bashan oaks, towering mountains and high hills. Manufactured things also are listed: military fortifications (v. 15), long-distance sailing ships (v. 16), and also humanity's own proud and haughty spirit (v. 17). The idols that humanity lifted up to worship in place of the true God also will be flung away in that day—no longer gods but food for the rats and bats (v. 20)!

Question 8. The Old Testament teaches that God is incomparable; he will not tolerate rivals; he will not share our allegiance. While human beings deliberately turn to other gods, they cannot receive God's forgiveness. The unforgiveable sin is the refusal to accept God's forgiveness.

Question 11. Food and clothing will be scarce (3:7), but what is emphasized is the lack of leadership (3:2) and society turning upside down (3:4-5, 12).

Question 12. Placing the fashion parade of 3:16 right next to the injustice of 3:15 sharpens our awareness of the divisions in society between rich and poor. What modern parallels can you think of?

Question 13. The "Branch" is a title of a very special person the Lord is going to send later (the Messiah); what begins as a general reference to new growth becomes focused in a Person (Jer 23:5; Zech 3:8).

Study 3. Isaiah 5. A Song of Injustice.

Purpose: To help us see what the consequences are of inconsistencies in our lifestyles personally and in our churches and nations.

General note. As you begin you may want to discuss briefly what a parable is and how it differs from an allegory in making, usually, one main point. It seems quite plausible to suggest that Isaiah introduced the message he wanted to give on this occasion by offering to sing a love song about a vineyard at a popular vintage festival. If this is so, we learn something about Isaiah's flexibility as a preacher, tailoring his message to fit the audience and situation. You may wish to compare the parable in this chapter to the parables in Mark 12:1-9 and Luke 13:6-9.

Structurally, this chapter falls into three sections: verses 1-7, 8-23 and 24-30, which are linked together by vintage or harvest imagery in verses 1-7, 10-12, 17, 22, 24. The chapter ends in deep darkness, providing a sharp contrast to chapter 6.

Question 1. Every conceivable care had been lavished on the vineyard: the site well-chosen and well-drained, the soil well-turned, the stones removed, pedigree vines planted. There was a watchtower to guard against thieves and a winepress hewn out of the rock. The owner had every right to expect a bumper crop.

Question 2. Could anything more have been done? If not, then what is the explanation? In verses 5-6 the disguise of the parable begins to slip, for Isaiah now uses first-person pronouns, and also by the end of verse 6 is threatening to withhold rain—and who but God could do that?

Question 3. There is a sudden change in rhythm in this verse and a very strong wordplay (in the Hebrew text) as Isaiah suddenly drops the disguise completely: God has lavished his care on Israel and Judah. Accordingly, he has looked for justice and righteousness. But what he has found is the rotten fruit of bloodshed and cries of distress.

Questions 6-7. Verses 8-10 describe property magnates. Verses 11-17 are about the self-indulgent. Verses 18-19 describe evildoers. In verse 20 those who overturn moral values are condemned. Verse 21 cites the falsely wise. Verses 22-23 describe the unjust.

The sins mentioned are mostly of those who are rich and influential, indifferent to property laws, drunkards, ignorant or careless of God's deeds and requirements, addicted to their evil practices, and moral relativists who measure everything by money.

Question 8. In chapter 2, Isaiah complained that the land was full of everything—but God. In verse 12 it again seems that the people have eyes for everything—except God. They cannot see his hand at work. Verse 24 sharpens the criticism. It is not that they are guilelessly ignorant, but that they are willfully so, rejecting God's law and spurning his word. There is a vivid contrast between this attitude and that of the nations streaming toward Jerusalem in 2:3.

Question 9. The expropriators will be cast out; their enlarged estates will produce catastrophically low yields; the gluttons will starve and the drink will dry up; death's appetite will prove even more voracious than their own (v. 14), indiscriminately swallowing all. God will reveal his justice and righteousness. The scene runs out in flying dust with corpses lying around like dung in the streets. The arm of God's anger is stretched out (v. 25).

Question 10. The Assyrian army approaches remorselessly, like a wild animal. Another picture occurs in 10:27-32. Compare the fearsome atmosphere of the words *Gestapo* or *Kempetai* or *Khmer Rouge* and the terror that they create.

Study 4. Isaiah 6. Responding to God's Call.

Purpose: To stimulate new or renewed responsiveness to God's awesome call on our lives.

Personal reflection. *Vocation* means calling—which implies a Caller. Is "career thinking" more appropriate to our culture today? Consider why the use of the term *vocation* is often restricted only to certain careers.

Question 1. King Uzziah had a long and prosperous reign. But in 2 Chronicles 26:16-21 we learn that when he was burning incense in the temple, the priests warned him against it because only they were permitted to burn incense. While Uzziah was arguing with them, he was afflicted with leprosy, which continued until he died.

According to Isaiah 1:1, Isaiah was called sometime before Uzziah's death. So why does he allude to Uzziah here? It may be because of Uzziah's throne being vacant. Here we see that God is still reigning on his throne even when the king is not.

Question 3. The seraphs' antiphonal song emphasizes the holiness of God and his glory. The message of God's holiness was especially relevant to Isaiah's careless, immoral society (see 1:4; 3:8; 4:3; 5:16). The song reminds Isaiah of God's nature, name and power. His glory, which is the outshining of his holiness, fills the whole earth. This is the background of Isaiah's messages to the nations (chapters 13—23) and of sayings like that in 11:9.

You may wish to compare the earthquake in the temple to the power of God's voice at Mount Sinai (Ex 19:16-19).

Question 5. We might expect Isaiah to be thrilled with what he saw, yet he was overwhelmed with a sense of his sinfulness and a certainty that seeing God would cause him to die. (For other such examples see Ex 33:20 and Judg 13:22.)

Why did Isaiah particularly mention "lips"? Perhaps because his call to be a prophet focused on his mouth. Or perhaps because what comes out of the mouth is a sign of what is going on in the heart (see for example Mt 12:34; Jas 3:2).

Question 6. Verses 6-7 show how the Holy One responds to contrition and humility. The action of the seraph looked threatening, but it was the means of forgiveness. The fire purifies. Then Isaiah is given assurance of his forgiveness.

Question 8. Up till now Isaiah has heard the seraph. Now he hears the Lord himself. Unlike Gideon, Moses, Jeremiah and others, Isaiah's response is unhesitating.

Question 9. Isaiah's audience could hear and see up to a point but without making the necessary response. Verse 10 makes explicit to Isaiah himself that the very clarity of his own preaching will make the people's blindness more inexcusable. Jesus (Mt 13:13-15) and Paul (Acts 28:26-27) also noted that rejecting a message makes hearing harder.

Question 11. God's answer to Isaiah's question about how long this state of affairs is to continue is that it will go on until the land is laid waste and a massive deportation ruins it. Ninety percent will be taken first, and then the remaining ten percent will again be devastated.

Isaiah lived through the destruction of the northern kingdom of Israel in 722 B.C. and predicted the destruction of the southern kingdom of Judah, which came about in 587 B.C. The last phrases of verse 13 have caused a lot of scholarly debate. The Good News Bible translates the last sentence, "The Stump represents a new beginning for God's people."

The picture is of the miracle of new growth. The tree (of God's people), though savagely mutilated and burned, shoots forth again. In contrast to the "seed of evildoers" (1:4 RSV)—as Isaiah describes his people—God will bring a holy seed. In Isaiah 11:1 we read, "A shoot will come up from the stump of Jesse; from his roots a Branch will bear fruit." This is reference to the Messiah who comes from David's line (David's father was Jesse).

Study 5. Isaiah 8:19—9:7. To Us a Child Is Born.

Purpose: To refresh our hearts with this astonishing prediction of what God's coming King would be like and to ask what effect this will have in our lives.

General note. If suitable to the context, you might begin this study with the chorus "For Unto Us a Child Is Born" from Handel's *Messiah*.

Question 1. Desperately looking for guidance, the people are turning to the spirits of the dead (necromancy) to learn about the future.

Question 2. Ahaz's political maneuverings have not been productive. As the awesome uncertainty of their position becomes increasingly plain, the people curse their king for getting them into this trouble and their God for not getting them out of it.

Question 3. Studying map 1 reveals that the region described includes upper and lower Galilee, the coastal plain and part of Transjordan, probably Gilead. Second Kings 15:29 shows that these areas had already fallen prey to the Assyrians before Ahaz's time. But in place of their gloom, distress and humiliation, and in place of their present condition, described only too accurately by the phrase "living in the land of the shadow of death," Isaiah predicts the dawning of a new and glorious day.

Question 5. The changes Isaiah predicts are glory for contempt (9:1), light for darkness (9:2), joy for sorrow (9:3), victory for defeat (9:4) and peace for war (9:5). In chapter 8 Assyrian strength seemed irresistible. But now there will be a wonderful victory like that of Gideon over Midian. The chafing yoke will be lifted, and the rod that beats them will be broken. **Question 6.** There are many possible answers. See for example John 1:46 and 7:52. Also consider the comments about Jesus' parentage, the saying that a prophet is not without honor except in his own country and Pilate sending Jesus to Herod. **Question 9.** It did not take place in the time of any Old Testament monarch. But everything begins to fall into place when a descendant of David is baptized and anointed with the Spirit and begins to preach in Galilee that the kingdom of God has arrived—although he refuses to allow the crowd to make him a political king. As for the last phrase of 9:7, it contrasts with human zeal, which fades out all too quickly. When God becomes enthusiastic to bring something about, there is no force in the universe that can stop him. **Question 10.** We live in a world in which God's bountiful resources are very unequally shared. This inequality is going to increase in the next twenty years because of massive population increases in the poorer countries. If those of us who are fortunate now do nothing or very little to bring about more justice and righteousness in the world, we will have reason to be nervous when God sets things right. But for those whose lives are a perpetual struggle for justice and righteousness, God's law and zeal will bring the peace we have been yearning for. **Question 11.** How can we be confused and distracted when we have a Wonderful Counselor? How can we be frightened and anxious when we have a Mighty God? How can we be lonely or time bound when we have an Everlasting Father? **Question 13.** The philosophy of history expressed by Isaiah is remarkable: even the most terrifying superpower of the age is an instrument in the hand of the Almighty God. We are not just in the grip of political and military forces that are beyond our control.

Study 6. Isaiah 11—12. A Hope to Live By.
Purpose: To enlarge and deepen our hope that there is a new world coming.
Group discussion. Introduce the study by brainstorming with the word *hope* and the ideas your group members associate with the word. Then compare and contrast the timbre of the word in modern speech with its use in the Bible.
Question 1. We have come across this analogy of a branch from a stump before—in 4:2 and 6:13. The person described is wise and discerning. He combines justice and power (which rarely go together). He combines ardor and reverence for God.

The New International Version translation of verse 3 is misleading: this person will, of course, use his eyes and ears! Phillips catches the meaning precisely: "He will not judge by appearances, he will not make decisions by hearsay." His judgments will mean life and joy for the poor but death for the wicked. The messianic King is fully equipped for his struggle with evil—with the best possible equipment of righteousness and faithfulness.

Question 4. People will likely find this to be an odd phrase as they pause to think about it. Suggest to the group that appropriate fear means "reverence and awe which issue in obedience." See Proverbs 1:9 where this is the first principle of godliness.

Question 5. Carnivores and herbivores will be each other's houseguests. Wild and domestic animals will feed together, led by an inexperienced child. Even the most ancient enmity between humanity and the snake will be removed. The new creation will share the character of the Prince of Peace.

Question 6. The church is meant to be a foretaste of Christ's kingdom of peace, but his designs are far wider than that: we want to see a transformed world!

Question 7. R. Pierce Beaver wrote of the seventeenth-century New England Puritans, "Men living in a relatively small community on the edge of an unexplored continent, remote from the great population centers, having some contacts with remote lands by sea trade but closely related only to the British homeland, having converted only a few hundred Indians, with one voice proclaim their certainty that the whole wide world belongs to Christ and is being brought to Him" (Iain Murray, *The Puritan Hope* [Edinburgh: Banner of Truth, 1971], p. 95). The danger of this type of thinking is an arrogant triumphalism. The danger of "the world will get worse and worse" view of the last things is an unbiblical pessimism.

Question 8. The nations rally to the banner of the Root of Jesse. The Lord reaches out his hand (terminology which is also found in Exodus) to bring his scattered people home. Isaiah 11:12 summarizes verses 10-11. The Lord will quench jealousy between Israel and Judah. They will destroy their enemies, and the saving journey home will be repeated. The theme of a new exodus is developed further in Isaiah 35 and 48.

Question 9. The Root is the Branch. The Root of David is also his offspring (Rev 22:16). The root deeply buried in the ground becomes the banner lifted high (11:10). The preexistent One enters time. Similarly, Jesus is crucified. He dies a demeaning, repellent death, yet attracts all to himself.

Question 10. Chapter 12 may be compared to the song of Moses in Exodus 15. The themes are praise, trust, fearlessness, thanksgiving and testimony.

Question 11. You may wish to conclude the study by singing one or two of several songs that are based on this chapter.

Study 7. Isaiah 24. Our Spoiled World.

Purpose: To study, in biblical terms, the price of physical and moral pollution now and in the end times.

Question 2. We tend to distinguish rather sharply between "natural" and "human" disasters. But perhaps the biblical picture of their interconnectedness is more appropriate than appears at first sight. But does it also seem to you from the insanity and cruelty of some conflicts and suffering that we human beings are in the grip of diabolical powers? Verses 21-22 point to the struggle between the supernatural powers, particularly with Satan and the fallen angels (v. 21). See also Ephesians 6:11-12.

Question 3. The last phrase of verse 4 states that the high and mighty do not escape this judgment. Verse 2 spells out the impartial universality of the ruin. Religious status, social status, economic status will make no difference.

Question 4. In the passage we see that the lights have gone out, a vast stillness is descending, and, in a piercing phrase of the RSV in verse 11, "All joy has reached its eventide."

Question 5. The optimist is inclined to shrug off this chapter's predictions as gloom and pessimism with the words "Surely it can't be as bad as all that!" The pessimist may be inclined to shrug his or her shoulders and say, "What can we do about all this? It is out of our control." Discuss the instability of each position.

Question 6. There are only two glimmers of hope—the "very few left" in verse 6 and the remnants of the olive and grape harvests in verse 13.

Question 8. The singing apparently arises from scattered remnants of God's people in the distant east and west. Of course, the day of judgment is for them the day of homecoming. In Revelation too we find that frequently through the smoke and flame and terror of the last days we can hear the sound of singing.

Question 9. As the chapter proceeds, the circle of judgment widens. In the earlier part attention focused on the social life of the inhabitants. But in verses 18-20 life itself is threatened by a disaster of the proportions of the flood in Noah's time. (Compare v. 18 with Gen 7:11.) With a very powerful wordplay in verse 19, Isaiah describes the earth rocking on its foundations. It rolls like a drunken man and sways like a flimsy watchman's shelter in a melon field (see Is 1:8).

Question 10. Verse 21 refers to the spiritual rulers of darkness in heavenly places and the kings who are their earthly counterparts. The brightness of God's revealed glory is such that the sun and moon pale by comparison. See Isaiah 60:19 and Revelation 21:23. God is taking his place as King on Mount Zion.

Question 11. This question points back to the group discussion. Some may have changed or revised their views. Conclude the study together with some silence, pondering the absolute reality of the words so often recited in the Nicene Creed: "He will come again in glory to judge the living and the dead, and his kingdom will have no end."

Study 8. Isaiah 25. Free at Last!

Purpose: To strengthen our faith by looking beyond our world's present and future devastation to God's coronation feast.

General note. Chapter 25 spells out some of the details of God's glory in one of the Old Testament's most memorable chapters. Structurally, we may see the passage 24:21—26:6 as a series of three messages followed by three short thanksgiving songs: God's judgment (24:21-23), God's protection (25:1-5), God's feast (25:6-8), God's salvation (25:9), God puts down the proud (25:10-12), and God lifts up the believer (26:1-6).

Question 1. God's perfect faithfulness experienced in the past is the pledge that he will carry out what he has promised and what he has threatened. "You have faithfully carried out the plans you made long ago" (TEV).

Question 2. The adjective *ruthless* is used three times in verses 3-5. Its use reveals that the main targets of God's leveling, subduing anger are the powerful, the prosperous, the oppressors and the godless.

Question 3. God, the impregnable stronghold for the poor and needy, is contrasted to the heap of ruins in verse 2. God's comprehensive protection in all circumstances is further illustrated by the extreme metaphors of the blast of a winter storm and the overpowering heat of a scorching desert wind (see, for example, 4:6). By a slight variation of the metaphor, God's intervention is compared to the shade of a cloud that cuts off the searing heat of the sun.

Question 4. As people share any recent experiences of bereavement, if the atmosphere becomes very loaded emotionally, take time to pray together.

Question 6. The mountain referred to in verses 6-7 and 10 is presumably Mount Zion (see 24:23). The richest food, the finest (well-aged) wines and the best meats (meat was not commonly eaten except by the rich—see Amos 6:4) are provided. All peoples are invited: it is not for Jews only. The covering shroud, or sheet, is either sorrow and mourning or blindness—or both. Death, the universal swallower, will itself be swallowed up forever. Tears will be wiped away—the tears of sorrow and the tears that follow contemptuous treatment. Then there will be deathless joy for all!

Question 8. Her end is pictured as that of a swimmer desperately trying to avoid drowning in a manure pit into which she has been ruthlessly thrown.

Question 9. See also Isaiah 16:6. Arrogant pride characterizes Moab. We may be sure that this is not just a biased anti-Moabite sentiment by reading Isaiah's cries of pain for Moab in Isaiah 16:9-11.

Question 10. You may also wish to refer to Matthew 22:1-14. Do not allow your group to be satisfied with the view that death doesn't matter for the Christian. This is a trivialization of death. How can we say that it does not matter that a person made in the image of God is reduced to food for worms?

It seems that Christians have, in fact, a view of death that is immeasurably brighter and darker: inextinguishable joy or irreparable loss. Nothing less.

Study 9. Isaiah 30:1-18. Who Can You Trust?

Purpose: To expose false objects of trust and to reinforce our trust in our Sovereign Lord.

General note. Isaiah chapters 28—33 include six messages from Isaiah to his society introduced by the word *woe.* The first of these messages is addressed to the northern kingdom of Israel. The last is addressed to Assyria (which is not named). The middle four messages are addressed to the kingdom of Judah. Most of these messages belong to the time of the Assyrian crisis in the reign of Hezekiah. The shadow of Assyria, the world power of the time, with its terrifying army, comes closer and closer in these chapters. In this situation, some people turned to alcohol. Others looked to Egypt as their only hope.

Question 1. The objections specifically mentioned are obstinacy, not consulting God and the stupidity of the whole exercise—trusting a useless ally.

Question 2. All Jews know the story of how God delivered them out of slavery in Egypt and led their ancestors into the Promised Land. Now Isaiah pictures the whole process reversed. Jews with animals heavily laden with gifts (which may be bribes) are trudging back through the southern Negev desert to Egypt. "Egypt!" says God contemptuously, "Dragon Do-Nothing!" "Rahab Sit-Still!"

Question 5. Rejection, oppression and deceit characterize the society (v. 12). It is rotten inside. Although the wall may look like fine protection from a distance, it is not secure. It will crack, bulge, and finally, it will collapse.

Question 6. The prophets are obstacles in the people's headlong rush to destruction. "Get out of the way!" they say (v. 11).

Question 9. The people are infatuated with the famous Egyptian cavalry. "With these horses we'll be able to get out of any situation," they say. "Yes," says Isaiah sarcastically, "they are excellent—for escaping!" In verse 17 Isaiah is using a similar technique to that used in verses 6-7. When the Israelites were on the way to the Promised Land, God gave them a promise that five of them would chase a thousand; a hundred would put ten thousand to flight (Lev 26:8; Deut 32:30). Now the situation would be reversed.

Study 10. Isaiah 36—37. The Source of Confidence.

Purpose: To observe Hezekiah and Isaiah at work in a major national crisis, and to learn to imitate their faith.

Question 2. He uses contempt (v. 5) and ridicule (v. 8). He estimates correctly the uselessness of Egypt as an ally (v. 6). He descends to vulgar threats (v. 12) and outright bluster (vv. 13-15).

Question 3. If Judah tries to claim the protection of Egypt, the commander will dismiss them as useless. If they claim the protection of the Lord, the commander is misrepresenting Hezekiah's reforms. He is trying to say they are defenseless.

Question 5. In verse 7 the commander cunningly misrepresents Hezekiah's reform. The altars Hezekiah destroyed were those often dedicated to Baal worship (see 2 Kings 18:1-7). In verse 10 he also distorts Isaiah's teaching about Assyria as God's instrument (see Is 10:5-6).

Question 6. In verses 16-17 he enticingly calls the exile a "journey to paradise." He finishes off in a roaring climax that draws a false conclusion (the Lord's helplessness) from undeniable facts (the destruction of other cities and other gods).

Question 8. The people kept quiet as the king had ordered. But it is clear from the officials' request in 36:11 and their reaction in 36:22 that they were at their wits' end.

Question 9. Clearly Hezekiah took the matter very seriously (37:1). Perhaps at last he sees the fruitlessness of turning to Egypt, which some of his officials were recommending (see chapters 28—33). Without presumption ("It may be," v. 4) he requests prayer.

Isaiah's reply is brief and pungent. The field commander is called an underling; his whole speech is labeled for what it really is—blasphemy. Isaiah tells of the Lord's promise to end the king's campaign and his life.

Question 10. Now at last it was time to mock the mocker. The Assyrian king was indeed a world conqueror, but he did not recognize who had planned it (37:26) or from whom his power derived. And for this reason, says Isaiah, using a vivid picture taken from Assyria's own brutal practice with those it conquered, God will take him home again (37:29). Isaiah finishes with the decisive repetition "He will not enter this city." When God defends, no attack can succeed (37:35). Conversely (see study 2), when God attacks, the sturdiest fortress fails.

Question 11. Sennacherib's campaign came to an abrupt and disastrous end. The corpses of 185,000 of his soldiers were left lying on the ground. Twenty years later (Isaiah is not interested in Sennacherib's intervening career) his own life came to an end—murdered by his own sons as he prayed to his god, Nisroch. Hezekiah prayed and his God heard; Sennacherib prayed but Nisroch was powerless to prevent his assassination.

In contrast, Hezekiah is offered a sign in 37:30-32 (like Ahaz). This year and next he will still suffer from the aftereffects of the world's most brutal army. But then things will return to normal. A remnant will remain (as Isaiah's son symbolized); God's zeal would ensure it (see Is 9:7).

Study 11. Isaiah 38—39. How Quick We Are to Forget.

Purpose: To recognize that God is a God who hears our prayers and answers them, but that we must continually listen for his voice as well.

General note. It seems clear from 38:6 that the events recounted in chapter 38 took place before those recounted in chapters 36—37. Verse 1 of chapter 39 makes it clear that chapter 39 follows chapter 38 chronologically. Why, then, were chapters 38—39 placed after 36—37? The most plausible answer appears to be as follows: chapters 36—37 are a very fitting climax to chapters 28—35 and the reign of Hezekiah. Chapter 39, however, is an excellent bridge to chapter 40 where the Babylonian exile is presupposed by the prophet. Chapter 39 reveals that it was the visit of the king of Babylon in Hezekiah's time that produced the prediction of 39:6 that everything would be carried off to Babylon. From 2 Kings 20:1-11 it appears that 38:21-22 belongs chronologically between 38:6 and 38:7.

Question 1. Isaiah's announcement to Hezekiah in verse 1 is meant to cause Hezekiah to recognize the real gravity of his situation. But God's purposes of salvation were not about to be extinguished by Hezekiah's premature death without a son. (Manasseh was only twelve when he began his reign, so presumably he was not born at this time.) After Hezekiah's prayer, Isaiah's rather prompt reply (see 2 Kings 20:4) is that God—the God of his father David—will spare and lengthen his life.

Question 2. Apparently somewhere in or near the king's palace were some steps called Ahaz's steps. The sun was already past its peak, and the shadow cast by some pillar or other object had already gone down ten of the steps. In the ordinary course of events there was no way the shadow could go back up again that day. The lengthening shadows of the dying day symbolize very vividly the passing of life. Hezekiah asked for the shadow to go back up again, which it did. Death was rolled back for another fifteen years! (For further details, see Bernard Ramm, *The Christian View of Science and Scripture* [Grand Rapids, Mich.: Eerdmans, 1954], pp. 110ff.; or *The International Standard Bible Encyclopedia*, ed. Geoffrey W. Bromiley et al. [Grand Rapids, Mich.: Eerdmans, 1979] 2:841ff.)

Question 4. The images include the prison gates of death clanging shut behind him (v. 10); death, the great robber (v. 10); the striking of a shepherd's tent (v. 12); the rolling up of a weaver's web (v. 12); and being cut off from the loom (v. 12). He feels as if he has been attacked by a half-ton lion (v. 13). He groans and murmurs (v. 14).

Question 5. Verse 18 is standard Old Testament language for the state of those who die under God's displeasure. But for those who die trusting in God there is a different story (see for example Ps 49:15; 73:23; 139:18).

Question 6. He recognizes God's overruling providence: "He himself has done this" (v. 15). He is assured that what had happened was for his benefit (v. 17). Just as gravity holds us on this whirling world, so God's love keeps us out of the pit (v. 17). God has forgiven him (v. 17). God is faithful (vv. 18-19).

Question 8. Second Chronicles 32:24-33 gives the most comprehensive account of Hezekiah's wealth, projects and death. Verse 25 mentions his pride, and according to verse 31, when the Babylonian envoys arrived, "God left him to test him and to know everything that was in his heart."

Question 9. Isaiah predicts the plundering of his treasures and the deportation of his own descendants to Babylon.

Question 10. Most people seem to think Hezekiah's reaction was complacent and self-serving: "At least I'm okay!" But E. J. Young thinks the words constitute "a child-like acknowledgement of the truth of the prophecy and also the mercy with which it is intermingled" (*The Book of Isaiah*, 3 vols. [Grand Rapids, Mich.: Eerdmans, 1965], p. 539).

Study 12. Isaiah 40. A Hope That Never Tires.

Purpose: To enlarge our knowledge of our wonderful, redeeming God and thus to fortify our souls against all adversities.

General note. You may wish to begin this study with appropriate music from Handel's *Messiah*. It could help to create a warm and expectant atmosphere for the group.

Question 1. The historical background of this chapter is important, especially the atmosphere of hopelessness of a refugee people in exile in Babylon. Forty years earlier there had been no one to comfort the stricken Jerusalem (Lam 1:2, 9, 16, 21). But although many might doubt it, Israel is still God's people, and he is still their God. God tells the prophet to speak tenderly but not in whispers—"proclaim." The message is threefold: her sentence has been served; the debt of her iniquity has been paid; she has been abundantly punished.

Question 2. The Bayeux tapestry in France has a picture of King William of Normandy prodding his soldiers into battle with his spear. The caption is "King William comforteth his soldiers." The prophet aims to invigorate and rouse his people from faithless lethargy as well as to speak tenderly to them. It is a fine balance.

Question 3. The road leads through the desert, westward from Babylon to Israel. Was this passage fulfilled by the return of the Jews from Babylon to Jerusalem? Yes, but it can also be seen as a passage with more than one fulfillment (See leader's notes, study 2, question 1). John the Baptist was the voice in the wilderness heralding the arrival of Jesus (Mt 3:1-5). The process of building highways to spread the good news of God's glorious coming in Jesus to all people still continues steadily.

Question 5. Human transience is here compared to the grass—scorched and shriveled in the desert wind. There is no good news here. The good news is in the eternal Word of God, the basis for our faith, as Isaiah tirelessly taught. Peter applies these tremendous words to the gospel as a basis for our life of love (1 Pet 1:23-25).

Question 6. God displays in verses 10-11 "the might of a ruler and the gentleness of a shepherd" (Christopher R. North, *The Second Isaiah* [Oxford: Oxford University Press, 1964], p. 79). The figure of a shepherd combines both because rulers were frequently called shepherds in ancient western Asia. Christopher North's translation illumines verse 10: "The Lord God is coming in might, with regal arm outstretched; with him are the sheep he has earned; they are his prize, and they march in his vanguard" (ibid., p. 33).

Question 7. It is unusual for a powerful person to combine both the attributes of power and gentleness. The metaphor of a shepherd (hard, dangerous work) is an appropriate one in this context. Encourage group members to speak specifically and not just in generalities.

Question 8. Our God exceeds any contrasting statements we can make about him. He is the Creator of all things, all-powerful and all-wise (vv. 12-14). He is the Lord of the nations (vv. 15-17) and their leaders and of history (vv. 21-24). He is the namer and controller of the stars and all astral powers (vv. 25-26). Astronomical space and geological time are as nothing to him.

Question 9. There is nothing malicious in these verses, and contemporary documents show that the picture they paint is not a caricature. Nevertheless, Isaiah does pour scorn on idolatry (especially in 44:9-20) and regards it as an abomination, something that the Lord detests (41:24; 44:19). How do we differentiate between grateful wonder at beautiful things and a faithless dependence on these things for our security?

Question 10. Some Babylonians worshiped the stars, but we worship their Creator.

Question 11. The complaint of the exiles in their despondency is that God does not see! God does not care! Isaiah replies that God is the Lord of time and space (v. 28); he does not lack power or wisdom (v. 28), and to the weary and the weak (even youths in full vigor sometimes fall exhausted) he will give new strength. Therefore, wait for him.

Question 12. Concern for poetic climax would probably have lead to the sequence *walk, run, soar.* But everyday life is not like that; soaring is occasional, but a lot of life is humdrum, and sometimes we come to a complete halt. In the "everydayness" of life we are also to find our hope constantly renewed in our God who never tires.

Question 14. The idols could not predict this turn of events, and they are useless at controlling it. There is a note of sarcasm in verse 7. The image is meant to be a god, but it has to be nailed securely so that it does not topple over. What use is such a deity?

Question 15. In verses 8-13 the Lord takes the hand of his frightened servant. In verses 14-16 the insignificant worm becomes a sharp threshing sledge. In verses 17-20 the parched desert traveler finds himself in a garden of Eden.

Study 13. Isaiah 42. "Here Is My Servant."

Purpose: To observe what God requires his servants to be and to do—a pattern fulfilled only by our Lord but to be followed by us.

General note. Chapter 41 introduced, in overpowering language, a foreign conqueror (later named as Cyrus, 44:28) who will deliver Israel out of its prison of slavery. Chapter 42, by contrast, speaks quietly of a yet more wonderful Deliverer, introduced anonymously by the Lord simply as his servant.

This passage is called a "servant song." There are several other servant songs in this section of Isaiah (see 49:1-50; 50:4-11; 52:13—53:12; 61:1-4), and they deeply influenced the mind and life of our Lord. He took for himself their main themes of complete obedience, fearless witness and undeserved suffering.

Question 1. The positive features of his appointment are (1) God has taken his hand to uphold, strengthen and support him; (2) God has chosen him for service; (3) God's favor rests upon him; (4) God's Spirit rests on him (Is 11:2).

Note seven negatives in the description of his character, which may be thus summarized: The servant is not sensational, thrusting, arrogant or military. He is steadfast and patient with others. North's translation of verse 4: "with faith undimmed and spirit unbroken he will establish my law"— reflects the fact that the words *undimmed* and *unbroken* are from the same root as *bruised* and *smoldering* in verse 3 (*Second Isaiah,* p. 109).

Question 3. Note who God is according to these verses: the Creator of all (v. 5), the covenant God (v. 6), the only God (v. 8), the Lord of history (v. 9). And note the verbs of which God ("I") is the subject and the servant ("you") is the object.

Question 4. The important ideas to discuss here are justice (vv. 1, 4), righteousness (v. 6), covenant (v. 6) and liberation (v. 7). It is a ministry that has kingly, prophetic and priestly aspects.

Question 5. The servant's ministry, as succeeding chapters make clearer, extends far beyond the borders of Israel.

Question 7. Many sincere Christians are only too conscious of their duty to serve the Lord, which they try conscientiously to fulfill. The more grateful they feel, the more the obligations pile up. It can be very exhausting. Ensure that you also take time to bask in the Lord's delight—his favor rests upon you!

Question 8. In verse 14 the picture abruptly changes to that of a woman in labor. To the exiles the Lord seemed to have been inactive for a long time. But now God is going to deliver his people. It is sad to note from verse 18 that those who are stuck in idolatry (v. 17) will not be led out.

This striking and violent language is of course metaphorical. Old Testament prophets spoke of a living, active God, not of an abstraction. We must not press metaphors too far. Only time would reveal that in accomplishing humanity's salvation it was God who would suffer the violence of humanity, rather than humanity who would suffer the violence of God!

Question 9. There is an oscillation in chapters 41—53 between the picture of Israel as God's servant (a task for which she proved unworthy) and the individual servant—a representative of Israel. The prophets are quite clear that the exile was not a political misfortune but a divine judgment (see Neh 9:6-38; Ps 106; Dan 9:1-49). This chapter, which starts with a thrilling picture of a dedicated and wise servant, ends in a bitter anticlimax, showing Israel as she actually is (v. 25).

Study 14. Isaiah 43:1—44:5. You Are Precious.

Purpose: To refresh, renew and restore our sense that we are highly valued by God.

General note. Structurally, the present passage falls into three sections: (1) God's abundant mercy (43:1-21), (2) Israel's unfaithfulness and consequent judgment (43:22-28) and (3) Israel's recommissioning as God's servant (44:1-5).

It might be suitable to begin the study by singing "Amazing Grace."

Question 1. In Isaiah 42:18-25 Israel is portrayed as a willfully blind servant. But her inconstancy is not reflected in God, whose "abounding grace" continues to pour out toward her. This is the meaning of grace—God loves us because he loves us, not because we deserve it.

Question 4. Israel is described in unflattering terms in verse 8 (see also 42:18-19). The foreign idols are interrogated in verse 9 and told to summon their witnesses. The Lord summons his witnesses in verse 10. They are to testify that he is the unique and only Savior, memorably and succinctly stated in verse 11. Isaiah's arguments against idolatry come to a scalding climax in chapters 45 and 46.

Question 5. The ships that were the objects of Babylonian pride, signs of their far-flung empire and prosperity, will be full of refugees fleeing from danger.

Question 6. Israel need not fear the mighty power of Babylon. They are to remember the mighty power of God rescuing his people from Egypt long ago at the time of the exodus. God can make a way through impassable obstacles (v. 16). He can utterly extinguish mighty armies (v. 17).

Question 7. A better translation of verses 18-19 can be found in North: "Let not memory linger over the past" (*Second Isaiah,* p. 42). Why not? Because God is going to do a new thing. He is going to rescue his people again. What he was in the past, he remains in the present: a saving God! Therefore, give praise to God (v. 21), for that is what we have been formed to do.

Question 9. The emphasis of verses 22-23 is that whoever it was whom Israel was going to such slavish lengths to worship, it certainly was not God! Yet verse 25 stands as one of the greatest Old Testament promises. God forgives because it is his very nature to do so.

The Lord also gives a deadly warning. The word *destruction* in verse 28 reminds us of the Israelite conquest of the Promised Land. (See, for example, Deut 13:15). If Israel is not careful, their whole history will be undone, and they will suffer the fate reserved for their enemies.

Question 12. The Jews returned from Babylon, but the promises of this chapter were not exhausted by that event. Acts records the pouring out of the Spirit and how Jews and Gentiles experienced the refreshing rain on a thirsty land. Yet there are still many living in literal and spiritual deserts who need to be brought to a knowledge of the living God. Each member of your group is infinitely precious in God's sight. Let each depart with this assurance.

Study 15. Isaiah 45. Turning to God.

Purpose: To grasp more strongly and gratefully the truth that God is the God of all time and space, and to accept the consequences that follow from this truth.

Group discussion. The philosophy called religious pluralism asserts that there are many culturally conditioned ways of access to ultimate reality (which some people call God), all of equal value. It is therefore arrogant and absurd, and probably ignorant, to claim that *my* way is the only way for all people.

Questions 1-2. The word *anointed* (later used technically as Messiah) is usually used in reference to kings in the Old Testament. God would use Cyrus as a deliverer. He would give Cyrus great wealth, even hidden treasures (which happened by Cyrus's conquest of the legendary Croesus, King of Lydia, and his conquest of Babylon).

Cyrus's own description of his conquests ascribes them to Marduk, god of Babylon, but he diplomatically restored other gods to their temples, which he allowed to be rebuilt. The Jews benefited from this enlightened policy (see v. 13 and Ezra 1:2-4), even though it appears that Cyrus's "knowledge" of the Lord (v. 3) was quite perfunctory (vv. 4-5).

The striking part of the interpretation of his conquests by Isaiah is that they are for the sake of Israel (which we may assume Cyrus scarcely noticed, being on the outermost western fringes of his empire) and, later, so that the whole earth (v. 6) may know the Lord. The rest of the chapter develops this theme. No wonder there is a hymnic outburst in verse 8 at the "marriage" of heaven and earth: vernal rains and lush earth join to produce righteousness, salvation, victory, prosperity and joy!

Question 3. The Bible refuses to countenance dualism—the view that there is an eternal slugging match between two ultimate powers. A high view of God's providence shaping and controlling the natural order, history and our personal circumstances gives deep stability to faith (see also Job 2:10 and Rom 13:6).

Question 5. It seems clear that at least some of the Jewish exiles felt that God was a bungler. Perhaps they were scandalized by Isaiah's teaching that Cyrus, a heathen king, was God's anointed. Verse 15 of this chapter may be an echo of complaints that God's ways are beyond our understanding.

God overrides this querulous attitude with a rebuke and a reassertion. Can the pot call its maker a handless idiot? Can a newborn infant criticize its parents? Can a mere human being order about the Creator of the whole universe? God is raising up Cyrus for his special purpose.

Question 6. If people's doubts are merely argumentative, a sharp rebuke may bring them to their senses. But if they arise out of deep agony, like Job's did, deep conversation may be more healing than quick rebuke—as Job's friends did not apparently realize (see Job 40—42).

Question 7. Verse 14 pictures foreigners coming to Israel in search of God. They come from beyond the fringes of even the widest Jewish empire of Old Testament times. They will make themselves Israel's captives, recognizing among them the presence of God.

Question 8. God is recognized as being with Israel (v. 14). He is the Savior of Israel (v. 18); there is no secret about this (v. 19). But this does not necessarily mean that Israel (or we) will fully understand God's ways; sometimes it is hard to see God at work (v. 15), as, for example, when Cyrus seems to be conquering the whole world, rather than the whole world turning to the Lord! It is important that we do not think that faith equals total knowledge; this, God has not promised us.

Question 9. The vision widens in verses 20-25 to the "ends of the earth" (v. 22). Ignorant idolatry of impotent gods is to be abandoned for the worship of the only true, living, saving, predicting God (vv. 20-21). Homage and worship are to be given exclusively to him (vv. 22-23). Shame will cover his opponents (v. 24), but Israel will be victorious.

Question 10. Because of humanity's dishonesty more than one witness is usually required in Jewish courts, and oaths (or promises) are permitted as a way of strengthening words. God's words need no strengthening—every word of his is a promise. He swears "by himself."

Question 12. God predicts that one day every knee will bow to him and every tongue will swear—not in profanity but in recognition and loyalty. These words, which God applies to himself in Isaiah, Paul applies, in his letter to the Romans, to Jesus. A Christian is not just an admirer or a follower or an imitator of Jesus, but a worshiper of Jesus.

Study 16. Isaiah 49:1-18. Strong Foundations for Service.

Purpose: To review the nature of the Lord's call and to encourage each other in his comprehensive love for us.

Question 1. When God calls, he names; he does not just shovel people into his business en masse. When he calls, he enables. A sharp sword is one that does its job; a polished arrow is one that flies truly to its target. God is a master craftsman—his consummate artistry is to be seen in the things and people he has fashioned!

Question 2. God has no unfinished projects. He is not taken by surprise by our unfortunate ancestry or temperament or choices. His call stretches far back behind all the decisions we have made, all the choices, all the mistakes. The golden chain of our salvation and usefulness runs all the way from his eternal foreknowledge to our final glory (see Rom 8:28-30).

Question 3. At first the servant is self-pitying: I have toiled; I am exhausted. But then he recalls that his vindication, his reward, is with God. Where could it be more secure! Some high-minded readers may flinch at this mention of reward. But Jesus, for example, gives us an incentive to put God's kingdom first in Matthew 6.33. What is it? What is important about rewards is whether they are appropriate to the endeavor. Money is not an appropriate reward for kindness. But justice is an appropriate reward for true service well-rendered.

Question 4. Verse 3 calls the servant Israel, but in verse 5 we see he has a ministry to Israel (and also in verse 6 to the Gentiles). Thus we conclude that the servant represents Israel—the ideal Israel.

God is going to display his glory in the servant's life and work. The job of a shepherd was a despised and unclean task in Bible times, but God is honoring the servant with the task of shepherding his people. Yet this task alone has too small a radius. The servant is also to be a light to lighten Gentiles (see 42:6), a theme picked up in Simeon's song (Lk 2:30-32) and in Acts 26:23. Thus, this chapter picks up themes that are developed in the later servant songs: on the one hand the servant is despised, abhorred, yet on other hand he becomes the object of universal homage.

Question 5. It is striking to note how the servant's memory turns to the time before he was born. In addition, the Lord enlarges the servant's vision to see God's salvation reaching to the ends of the earth. Here is a cure for despondency. Kings and rulers (and journalists) may despise us; the people we seek to serve and challenge may not jump up with enthusiasm for the vision that we put before them. But our call in the remote past and our vindication in the future help us to press on.

Question 6. Various aspects of the servant's ministry are mentioned in verses 7-12: transformation—slavery to honor (v. 7); restoration—ruins to reconstruction (v. 9); release—prison to freedom (v. 9); provision—hunger to pasture (vv. 9-10); guidance (vv. 11-12).

Question 7. The exodus is the Old Testament event most commonly referred to in the New Testament. There are many echoes of that event in verses 8-12 and in the ministry of our Lord.

Verse 6 says literally that the servant is to "be my salvation to the ends of the earth." Salvation is not a concept; it becomes a person in our Lord. He is the embodiment of God's promises of light, liberation, provision and pity. Verse 12 pictures pilgrims returning to Zion from the most distant parts, of which Aswan (Sinim) is a representative. Hudson Taylor thought this verse referred to China (cf. "Sinologist"). But probably today we would say something like "from Timbuktu"!

Question 8. When the full gathering in of all God's people takes place, then will be the time for unceasing songs (Rev 7:9-12). Every interim gathering, wherever it happens, is a foretaste, a pledge of yet more wonderful comforts and compassions yet to come.

Question 9. It is easy to lose sight of God's blessings when caught up in the troubles of the moment or daunted by the size of the task you are facing. Zion grumbles that the Lord has forgotten. But he renews his promise: I can no more forget you than a nursing mother can forget the child she nurses. Your name is tattooed indelibly on my hands. I see your walls constantly before my eyes (as a refugee longs for home).

Study 17. Isaiah 52:13—53:12. The Burning Heart of Scripture.

Purpose: To meditate on the sufferings of the servant of the Lord, who is Jesus Christ, and to respond with grateful adoration.

General note. It is a striking fact that Isaiah 40—66 divides into three groups of nine chapters: 40—48, 49—57 and 58—66 (see refrains in 48:22 and 57:21 for confirmation). Of the middle section, 49—57, chapter 53 is the middle chapter. This passage, 52:13—53:12, has five stanzas, of which 53:4-6 is the middle one. In the stanza 53:4-6, the middle verse is 5. It is set like a diamond in concentric circles of wonder.

Question 1. Isaiah 52:13-15 poses a number of acute textual problems that may surface if group members have different Bible versions. Do not get hijacked into too much argument about these.

It is clear that people are appalled at the servant's disfigurement; he almost seems subhuman. Yet it appears that he has some sort of priestly ministry, an unexplained sprinkling that leaves kings and rulers dumbfounded.

Question 2. God is going to exalt his servant to where he himself is (see 6:1). It is almost certain that Acts 2:33 is reminiscent of this passage; the apostles saw the experience of Jesus mirrored in this chapter. Although he was opposed, rejected and crucified by humanity, God had lifted Jesus to the very highest place!

Question 3. When God acts to save, the person who appears is not a Rambo-style figure, a James Bond escapologist specializing in miraculous rescues. But it would also be a mistake to interpret these predictions as meaning that the Deliverer would be physically repulsive. The main feature of verses 1-3 seems to be lack of recognition.

Question 4. We thought that this man was under God's judgment for his own sins. But no! God laid on him our sins. We have selfishly chosen our own way rather than God's. And the judgment we deserve has fallen on him. Verse 5 summarizes it precisely and passionately:

> He was pierced
> for our transgressions,
>
> He was crushed
> for our iniquities,
>
> His punishment
> brings us peace,
>
> By his wounds
> we are healed. (author's translation)

The atonement (God's way of putting us right with himself through Jesus Christ's death) itself, not our explanations of it, is what saves us. An infinite number of hymns have been written about this—perhaps singing is more appropriate than arguing about how it works! Rebellions, failures, disintegration and woundedness characterize *us*. He, the Servant, was pierced, crushed, punished, wounded. It is the word *for* that establishes the relation between these two realities. What he did, he did *for us*.

Question 5. We read of his quiet attitude in face of harsh treatment; his arrest and sentence; how he was led away with no supporters left; how he was executed like a criminal, yet buried "with a rich man," although he had done no wrong. The particularities of the parallels are astonishing.

Question 8. There at least five allusions to Isaiah 53 in these verses: (1) compare 1 Peter 2:22 with Isaiah 53:9; (2) compare 1 Peter 2:23 with Isaiah 53:3; (3) compare 1 Peter 2:24 with Isaiah 53:12; (4) compare 1 Peter 2:24 with Isaiah 53:5; (5) compare 1 Peter 2:25 with Isaiah 53:6.

Question 9. Peter, like many Christians, must have naturally thought of Isaiah 53 when he wanted to explain the meaning of Christ's death and also when he wanted to highlight our Lord's behavior as a model for his followers.

Question 10. The crucial word in Isaiah 53:4 is *for*. The verse says that "he" was pierced, crushed, punished and wounded. This is a historical fact. The verse also mentions our rebellions, our failures and our sick, disintegrated lives. These facts can be seen clearly in our lives today. The word *for* connects these two facts. This is the heart of the Bible's salvation story.

In this chapter we stand as mice before a mountain; we see the uttermost lengths and depths that God in his love goes for us. Here is analgesic for our deepest pains; medicine for our sorrows. We do not believe in the infinite iceberg of metaphysics. We trust in a God who laid aside his immunity to pain, who has experienced fatherlessness and sonlessness.

Study 18. Isaiah 54—55. Shout for Joy.

Purpose: To arouse hope and zeal as the group gains a vision of God's purposes for his people and the invitation he extends to all.

General note. There are two major metaphors in chapter 54. The reference of both is first of all Jerusalem, or Zion, the holy city personified, and second, the exiled Jews in Babylon with all their deferred hopes. But the New Testament applies the vision to the church as it is and, most gloriously, to the church as it will be when salvation will be complete.

Question 1. The barren, childless woman is Zion. She was married to the Lord (see Jer 2; Hos 2), but because of her sins she has been forsaken (49:14), bereaved (49:20) and estranged (50:1).

Question 3. It may be that there are group members who are going through a hard time at this moment who do not feel the richness and closeness of God's love at present. If discussion shows this to be the case, it may be appropriate to pray for them right now. In this appropriate way, talk *about* God passes immediately into talk *to* God. How impertinent it is for us just to talk about God and not remember that without his presence by his Spirit we could not even draw one breath.

Question 4. An afflicted, storm-lashed, disconsolate, desolate city will be rebuilt in startling, costly beauty. This is the original of a yet more magnificent vision in Revelation 21:19. But the true beauty of the city is not its sparkling architecture but its character. It will be a place of discipleship, of godliness and prosperity, a place of righteousness, rejecting tyranny and terror. Immunity from attack is not promised, but final vindication is.

Question 5. The answer to the question is "Yes!" The first fulfillment was that historical Jerusalem was rebuilt. Jesus applied verse 13 to the disciples (John 6:45), and Paul applies verse 1 to the church (Galatians 4:27). We are the Jerusalem whose members have been born from above. The old tent of Judaism has been stretched to cover the whole earth. And where more clearly and piercingly than at the cross do we see God's overflowing and everlasting love? Thus these verses apply to the gospel age today. But there is a future application too, outlined in Revelation 21, when the church will be united, beautiful, holy, all-glorious and complete. Then will take place the marriage super of the Lamb. These verses fill our hearts with longing and eager expectancy for that time.

Questions 7-8. There are two climaxes in chapter 55. First, hungry people need satisfaction; verses 1-5 show the journey from poverty to abundance and mission. Second, wicked people need salvation, and verses 6-13 show the journey from sin through pardon to glory.

Repentance, says Derek Kidner, challenges "the mind . . . and the will, the habits (*ways*) and the plans (implied in the Heb. for *thoughts*). It is both negative (*forsake*) positive (*return,* or simply *turn*), personal (*to the Lord*) and specific (for *mercy*)" ("Isaiah," p. 664). Additionally, the appeal is reinforced by the shortness of the time (v. 6) and the abundance of the promise (v. 7).

Question 9. God's thoughts of forgiveness are higher than humanity's thoughts of revenge. God's words are productive, not empty (vv. 10-11). This is a reason for celebration with the whole creation (v. 12). Released captives and a transformed world will be indestructible symbols, signs of grace abounding (v. 13).

Chapters 56—66 go on to speak in greater detail about the transformation of the homeland, a place of corruption (56:9—59:15) and the devastation (63:7—64:12) into a "crown of beauty for the whole earth" (60—62).

Study 19. Isaiah 61. Jeans of Joy & Shirts of Praise.

Purpose: To understand the basis of encouragement so that we can better minister to each other.

General note. Although the word *servant* is not found in this passage, it is customary to align the passage with the four earlier servant songs with which it shares several common themes. The servant is both a kingly and prophetic figure, and of course the manifesto of verses 1-3 beautifully suited our Lord's ministry in the spirit of the Beatitudes.

Question 2. These verses describe a revolutionary ministry. We must not underemphasize the note here of "righteousness" and "justice," but John the Baptist (for example) had to discover that in his case the "opening of prisons" was spiritual (see Lk 7:18-23).

Question 3. As you discuss the metaphors in verse 3—"oil of gladness," "garment of praise" and "oaks of righteousness"—you will find them much more energetic than straightforward factual statements. Metaphors make truth not only clear to the understanding but also glorious to the imagination.

Question 4. Job complained that his friends (falsely called comforters) spoke to him "proverbs of ashes" (Job 13:12). Their words did not come from their hearts to his heart; they were just windbags. Encourage the group to press beyond mere discutsion of ideas to mutual ministry.

Question 5. *Exegesis* means the drawing out of the meaning of a text. What will be the most effective exegesis of the gospel to those who do not yet understand it? Not just the clarification of its *meaning,* but a display of its *beauty* in the lives of those who live by it. We are to exegete the gospel by our lives.

Question 6. Ruins will be rebuilt and citizens will return. Immigrants will serve in various tasks. Israel will fulfill a priestly role. Wealth will flow in from former plunderers. Israel had received a "double punishment" (40:2); now she will receive the "double portion" of the firstborn son. Their fame will spread abroad, and they will be recognized as a people blessed by the Lord.

Question 8. The fulfillment of this prophecy (and similar ones in 14:1-2 and 60:4-16) outran the terms of the predictions. Gentiles poured into the church that knew no national boundaries. All Christians are kings and priests to God. Human pride is brought low before the Lord, and all his people are the beneficiaries of his everlasting covenant.

Question 9. The "robe of righteousness" (compare the "best robe" of Luke 15:22) is a gift, an undeserved present. The sprouting seed of righteousness grows up from the soil. God's people receive the unmerited gift of righteousness; they also make every effort to do what is right. In both cases the Lord is at work: "Every virtue we possess, and every duty done, and every thought of holiness are His alone" (Harriet Auber, "Our Blest Redeemer, Ere He Breathed His Tender, Last Farewell").

Question 10. *Righteousness* sounds abstract and theological. Translate it "justice, what is good and right," and it appears in practical, everyday working clothes. We are "counted righteous" before God on the basis of Christ's death alone; our good deeds acquire us no merit. But our active everyday goodness is to be the evidence of delighted gratitude to God for what we have received.

Question 11. Many answers are possible. But if joy is anchored firmly in the Lord (v. 10), then even in dark times (as in Revelation) songs will break out again and again. Negro spirituals mitigated the great evils of slavery. Paul and Silas sang songs of praise at midnight in the Philippian jail. It seems that praising is good for you!

Study 20. Isaiah 62. The Exhilaration of God's Love.

Purpose: To participate in the delight of Zion renamed and restored, and to share the exhilaration of God's love for us.

Group discussion. Basic facts about refugees are at <www.oneworld.org/guides/migration/>. There are, of course, many different reasons why people leave their homes.

Question 2. It is possible that the speaker in verses 1-5 is God, but it also makes sense to assume that it is Isaiah speaking (he is certainly the speaker in chapter 64). Here he reveals the motive of his whole prophetic ministry: Zion's righteousness and salvation.

Question 3. The mystery of God's unquenchable love for Zion is baffling for many in this age of safe investments, limited liability and prenuptial contracts. The Old Testament does not explain this mystery (the nearest we get to an explanation is Deut 7:7-8), but it is content to state and restate it. One could say that the whole Bible is a development of this theme.

The book of Lamentations expresses the agony of Jerusalem's destruction: raped, deserted and (apparently) futureless. We catch an echo of that despair in 49:14. But now righteousness and salvation and glory are to replace wickedness, judgment and shame. Zion is to have a new name like a bride; she is to be a splendid crown in God's hand. The metaphor takes a surprising turn in verse 5, but the meaning is clear: "the godly are as much wedded to as produced by their mother-city" (Kidner, "Isaiah," p. 668).

Question 4. The restoration of Zion will take place in full view of the nations and their rulers (v. 2). Thus, the Lord will manifest his glory and confound those who assumed that Jerusalem was destroyed because Marduk, the Babylonians' god, was more powerful than Jehovah.

Question 5. The Christian doctrine of God's impassibility does not mean that God is unfeeling. It means that the infinite joy that overflows from the bright land of the Trinity cannot be diminished by the distresses and sorrows that he voluntarily enters. The dog in the manger will not have the last word in history. God's delight and exultation in us, his people, is supposed to arouse a corresponding commitment in us.

Question 6. Jerusalem's watchmen, her prophets, are unflatteringly described in 56:10. Their real purpose is to awake Jerusalem to the news of the messenger who is coming (see 52:8). According to these verses, not only are they to have nights of prayer, but they are also to give God sleepless nights!

Question 7. The unconditional security solemnly promised Israel by the Lord is another example of a promise that has been partially fulfilled—in 539 B.C. and (according to some) in A.D. 1948, but it has not yet been *fully* realized. We can see today very clearly how the security of Israel affects the security of the whole world.

Question 8. It is time to leave Babylon. We can almost see the procession assembling: The gates are open. Get ready! Clear the road! Remove any obstacles! Raise the banner! The march is ready to begin.

Question 10. When a craftsman finishes a project, the completed article is the "recompense" (or "fruit of his work"), and his pay is his reward. "In the case of the Anointed One, his saved people are both what he has earned and what he has accomplished; in terms of 53:12, both his portion and his spoil" (J. A. Motyer, *The Prophecy of Isaiah* [Downers Grove, Ill.: InterVarsity Press, 1993], p. 508).

Study 21. Isaiah 63:7—64:12. A Cry for Forgiveness & Revival.

Purpose: To enlarge our understanding and practice of prayer by studying Isaiah's famous prayer for revival.

Group discussion. J. I. Packer has summarized what happens in times of revival as follows: "God comes down; God's Word comes home; God's purity comes through; God's people come alive; outsiders come in" (*Keep in Step with the Spirit* [Leicester, U.K.: Inter-Varsity Press, 1984], p. 244).

Question 1. Isaiah does not plunge into petition. He begins by recounting God's past mercies. If we did this more, our prayers might be more passionate.

Additionally, notice the number of question marks throughout the passage. Prayer is not meant to be a formal ritual. Here it is a lively, passionate interview that is concluded with God's answers in chapters 65-66.

Question 2. Isaiah's prayer was informed by his knowledge of Israel's past. There are various allusions to the time of the exodus and judges (see, for example, Ex 3:7; 19:4; 23:20-23; 33:14; Judg 10:16). The warmth of the passage can scarcely be exaggerated. Fatherly hopes, redeeming love, presence, distress, love, mercy and faithfulness are expressed.

Question 3. Even in the worst of times there are things for which we should thank God. If we cannot see him in our present circumstances, there are always past mercies to bring a sense of proportion to present troubles. Sometimes, of course, the remembrance of the past makes present trials seem more acute. Thus, praise and petition interact and reinforce one another.

Question 4. Israel was, of course, familiar with the truth of God fighting for them (see, for example, Ex 14:14; Josh 10:14). The thought that God might fight against them (most clearly stated in Jer 21:5) was an unpalatable, therefore forgotten, truth. Clearly, however, grief and anger are not incompatible. As a Russian priest once said, "Love and anger were the world's redemption."

Question 6. Perhaps every culture attempts to domesticate its gods so that they become comfortable to live with. It would appear that many modern Westerners think of God as pure benevolence, a Santa Claus in the sky. We have forgotten his power and his holiness. But salvation in the Bible takes place against the background of God's unfathomable love *and* his revulsion from all that is evil.

Question 7. All over the world one of the major problems that worshipers of gods face is the unpredictability of the gods' behavior and demands. How can one be sure that one has behaved correctly, offered the right sacrifices, carried out the desired rituals and so on? But the God of the Bible is different. Catherine of Siena said that there is only one fire in God: the fire of his love to all burns in blessing on those who turn *to* him and in judgement on those who turn *from* him.

Question 9. Externally, enemies have trampled the sanctuary (63:18), the sacred city is deserted (64:10) and God's glorious temple is a blackened ruin (64:11). But the internal, individual symptoms are worse: rebelliousness and persistent hardness (63:17; 64:5). Isaiah 64:6 brilliantly portrays sin's power to imprison, deprave and disintegrate. In the end apathy rules (64:7).

Question 10. What is striking in Isaiah's prayer is how passionately he pleads for divine intervention. The only way of escape from divine judgement is to find the way of escape that God has fatherly provided.

Study 22. Isaiah 65:17—66:24. The Terror & the Glory.

Purpose: To energize our faith and love by dwelling on Isaiah's hopeful vision of the new heavens and the new earth.

Personal reflection. This is perhaps a hot topic for those brought up to believe that God is pure benevolence. If we recognize righteous anger, it would appear logical to believe that a perfect righteousness would include a perfect anger, a controlled but unappeasable revulsion from all that is evil.

Question 1. Observe the verbs of which God is the subject in verses 17-19 and 24. The tone of promise is this-worldly: the healing of memories (v. 17), joy (v. 18) and long life (vv. 20-23) are included. The last verses of the chapter echo 11:6-9, reminding us that this is the Messiah's kingdom.

Question 2. People complain when believers talk about "pie in the sky when you die." Here we have a typical example of expressing the inexpressible and visualizing the unseen in the only possible way—namely, in terms of what we already know. Of course, the reality will far transcend the description here. Our trouble in speaking of heaven is heaven's excess of reality, not lack of it.

Question 5. God commanded the rebuilding of the temple, but he cannot be contained in it (66:1-2) as some worshipers would like to do.

Question 6. God is looking for humble, penitent, awestruck worshipers. The worship of those mentioned in verse 1 is characterized by unreality (v. 3), indifference (v. 4) and sarcastic criticism (v. 5). The Good News Bible clarifies the meaning of verse 3: "The people do as they please. It's all the same to them whether they kill a bull as a sacrifice or sacrifice a human being; whether they sacrifice a lamb or break a dog's neck."

Question 8. Isaiah 66:7-11 is the last of several songs in these chapters of Isaiah portraying Zion as wife and mother. These verses emphasize the dramatic suddenness of her children's "arrival," the fact that God will certainly finish something that he has begun (compare v. 9 with Hezekiah's question in 37:3), and the joy of a mother and the abundant satisfaction of a nursed child. One day the difficult days of pregnancy will be over, the trauma of delivery will be past, and we shall inhabit a new world.

Question 9. The negatives mentioned are fury, fire and sword (66:14-16), the undying worm, and the quenchless fire (v. 24).

Question 10. The positive elements are peace, prosperity and consolation (66:12-13), Jewish exiles and refugees pouring toward Jerusalem from earth's remotest corners (66:19-21), and, finally, a new heaven and a new earth, and endless joyful worship from an international multitude (66:22-23).

Howard Peskett is vice principal at Trinity College, Bristol, England, where he teaches mission and religion. He served with Overseas Missionary Fellowship in Singapore for twenty years.